MEXICO'S
VOLCANOES

MEXICO'S VOLCANOES

A CLIMBING GUIDE

SECOND EDITION

R. J. Secor

THE MOUNTAINEERS

© 1981, 1993 by R. J. Secor

7 6 5 4 3
5 4 3 2 1

Published by The Mountaineers
1011 SW Klickitat Way, Seattle, Washington 98134

Published simultaneously in Canada by Douglas & McIntyre, Ltd., 1615 Venables Street, Vancouver, B.C. V5L 2H1

Published simultaneously in Great Britain by Cordee, 3a DeMontfort Street, Leicester, England, LE1 7HD

Manufactured in the United States of America

Edited by Heath Lynn Silberfeld
Cover design by Lynne Faulk
Book layout by Nick Gregoric
Typography and book design by The Mountaineers Books
Drawings by Dee Molenaar
Line maps by Karen Lemagie and Brian Metz/Green Rhino Graphics
All photographs by the author unless otherwise noted

Cover photograph: Popocatépetl from Iztaccíhuatl

Library of Congress Cataloging in Publication Data
Secor, R. J.
     Mexico's volcanoes / R.J. Secor. -- 2nd ed.
          p.   cm.
     Includes index.
     ISBN 0-89886-329-5
   1. Mountaineering--Mexico--Guidebooks. 2. Volcanoes--Mexico--
Guidebooks. 3. Mexico--Guidebooks. I. Title.
   GV199.44.M6S42   1994
   917.2--dc20   93-4383
                                                CIP

CONTENTS

ACKNOWLEDGMENTS

Second Edition

I am extremely grateful for the help I received from the following individuals in Mexico: Gerardo Reyes, Francisco Reyes, José Amador Reyes, Enrique Ramírez Juárez, Manuel Gutierrez, Joaquin Canchola L., Alberto Daiz Galicia, Daniel Méndez Franco, and Roberto H. du Tilly. And I am especially grateful for the assistance I received from Hector Luis Ruiz Barranco of the Mexican National Park Service, who notified park personnel of my visits in advance, providing me with information on Mexico's volcanoes that I never would have obtained on my own.

And I want to thank the following individuals from the United States for their route information, experiences, and genuinely constructive criticism, which made the second edition of this modest volume much stronger: Kurt Wedberg, Jerry Thompson, Ed Wilson, Winston Crausaz, Jimmy Katz, Mark Adrian, and Tony Bird.

It is a common, but preposterous, myth that an author of a mountaineering guidebook gets to spend all of his or her time in the mountains discovering the secrets that they hold. In reality, about half of the author's time is spent in places other than the mountains, talking to other climbers to discover the secrets of the mountains. And my climbing partners who have been with me on Mexico's volcanoes know this all too well. On more than one occasion I sipped a cool drink while deep in conversation with a new friend, completely oblivious to the plight of my companions who were sweltering in the hot sun. But they were good sports, even while I was leading them to the edge of an abyss in an attempt to follow a "better" route, or promising sunshine in January and delivering snow. I want to thank the following individuals for never losing their sense of humor, and understanding that the mountaineering guidebook author's work is never done: Mitch Halbricht, Scott Sullivan, Graham Breakwell, Rick Beatty, Ron Matson, Dave Petzold, Mario Gonzalez, and my father, John Secor.

And I want to thank the publishing staff of The Mountaineers, under the direction of Donna DeShazo, for their longtime support of my climbing guidebooks. It is fortunate that the editorial manager, Margaret Foster, selected Heath Lynn Silberfeld to serve as this book's editor. Heath's skill as an editor combined with her knowledge of Spanish and English made me look good. Helen Cherullo oversaw the production responsibilities, with the help of Storm Yanicks, Rick May, Christine Clifton-Thornton, and Marge Mueller.

First Edition

Herb Kincey critically reviewed the text and provided photographs.

Zell Rust and Gloria Carlson reviewed and corrected my Spanish. I take full responsibility for any remaining errors.

Otis McAllister provided the bulk of the historical information, and it is regrettable that he passed away before this book came into print.

John Pollock helped get this book started, and Ann Cleeland took on editorial responsibilities; I am very grateful for their tolerance and persistence. Donna DeShazo deserves credit for the fine collection of maps and photographs.

PREFACE

Second Edition

When the first edition of this book appeared in 1981, I never expected Mexico to undergo such a radical change within the span of ten years. Up until the mid-1980s, the Mexican government maintained the nationalist model that it inherited from the 1910 revolution—a protected, state-run economy where imports and foreign investment were blocked. This model is now out, having been replaced by the free market. The change has been remarkable. The annual growth rate of the national economy now has a solid foundation. The national deficit has now been eliminated. Inflation is now under control. And billions of dollars of foreign investment have poured into the country, along with lots of imported goods. The Mexican stock market soared in the early 1990s, so much so that comparing it to the American stock market made Wall Street look like a catatonic tortoise. Up until the mid-1980s, stores in Mexico featured domestically made second-rate appliances and televisions. A national joke called these "Mabe" appliances; maybe they worked and maybe they didn't. These same stores are now stocked from floor to ceiling with Japanese compact disc players, Korean microwave ovens, and U.S.-made refrigerators. And the Mabe appliances now compare favorably with their non-Mexican competition. In the late 1970s, one could look out during the pre-dawn hours from high on El Pico de Orizaba and see a dark countryside. Now, one can literally see a thousand points of light, the visual results of a successful rural electrification program. The jeep drivers that serve climbers on El Pico de Orizaba now have telephones that work, and one of them even has a fax machine to take reservations from climbers!

Mexico is now a developed country, and all of this progress has started to affect the high volcanoes. Semi-trucks now drive through villages whose historic buildings survive earthquakes but not the almost continuous vibrations of heavy vehicles. Paved roads are slowly creeping up the formerly "wild" east slope of El Pico de Orizaba. These roads will ease the access to this side of the mountain for climbers, but will also increase the access for development. Villages will increase in size, and fields of potatoes and other crops will replace the formerly exquisite forests. Cattle, goats, and sheep will graze higher on the slopes, and this may result in vast amounts of erosion. The eastern slope of El Pico de Orizaba has the most diverse climatic zones of any location in North America, with equally diverse plants and animals. It will be interesting to see how this development will be managed in the next decade.

One change that is especially heartening is the reduction of litter on

El Pico de Orizaba from Coscomatepec

Mexico's volcanoes. This problem has not been entirely eliminated, but the volume of trash that was once common is now rarely seen. What is interesting is that climbers, both Mexican and foreign, did this themselves, with no coercion from government authority. Mountaineers share with everyone the responsibility for conservation, and in Mexico, at least, climbers are setting the example.

But some things never change. A party of North American climbers once made their camp near a village high on El Pico de Orizaba. Just before sunset, the villagers visited the climbers, and insisted that they strike their camp and stay in their homes that evening. After a hearty dinner and breakfast the North Americans reluctantly left their new friends, leaving behind a supply of crayons and small toys for the children of the village. I am continually amazed by the reciprocity of kindness that is shared by our two cultures.

R. J. Secor
Pasadena, California
May 1992

First Edition

The number of Americans visiting Mexico's volcanoes has increased greatly over the past ten years. It is my hope that this slim guide will add to the enjoyment of those exploring the alpine regions of Mexico.

There is much more to Mexico than its mountains. Each city, town, and village has a special character of its own, and the foreign visitor who doesn't make the effort to uncover these unique attributes will return with little more than a "peak-bagging" experience. Most Mexicans are friendly, courteous, and willing to offer assistance to the best of their ability; they set an excellent example for other people of the world.

In a similar vein, the foreign visitor should set a good example so that future visitors will be welcome. Tourists must respect the property of others and leave wild areas in their natural state. The climber's concern for the alpine environment of the volcanoes may help encourage other tourists and local residents to leave these great peaks without blight. Let us not allow increased usage of the high volcanoes to lead to environmental costs.

This guidebook is not a substitute for mountaineering skill, experience, or judgment. The tourist routes on these mountains may appear simple, but several insidious dangers are always present on these volcanoes. Inexperienced mountaineers are urged to take advantage of instruction and training provided by various mountaineering clubs before attempting any high mountain ascent.

R. J. Secor
Pasadena, California
June 1981

A Note About Safety

The author has provided important tips on safety in this book. In addition, he and the publisher have taken all reasonable measures to ensure the accuracy of the route descriptions contained herein. Even so, routes vary greatly in difficulty and in the amount and kind of experience and preparation needed to enjoy them safely. Mountaineering entails certain unavoidable risks, and routes may have changed after this book was written. A route that is safe in good weather or for a highly conditioned, properly equipped climber, may be completely unsafe for someone else or under adverse conditions. There is not space in this book for a general discussion on climbing, but there are a number of good books and public courses on the subject, and you should take advantage of them to increase your knowledge.

Current political conditions also may add to the risks of travel in Mexico in ways that this book cannot predict. For these reasons, the descriptions in this book are not guarantees that a particular trip will be safe for you or your party. When you take a trip, you assume responsibility for your own safety. Keeping informed about current road conditions, weather changes, and political developments, and utilizing your common sense, are keys to a safe, enjoyable tour.

The Mountaineers

INTRODUCTION

Two mountain ranges traverse the Mexican republic roughly from north to south. The eastern chain is the Sierra Madre Oriental and is characteristically of low relief and lacking in prominent peaks. The Sierra Madre Occidental serves as the western range and forms a land barrier between the Pacific Ocean and the interior of the country. It averages 3000 meters (10,000 ft) in elevation, covers a greater area, and is much more rugged than the Sierra Madre Oriental. It is an arid region and is seldom visited. Aside from a few towns and mines, there are scant means of access. For the hiker, the main attractions of this area aren't the mountains, peaks, or ridges, but the canyons created by rivers that rush down the western slope into the Pacific and the Gulf of California. Quite often the vertical relief exceeds 1500 m (5,000 ft). A case in point is the Urique River, which cut the Barranca de Cobre southeast of Chihuahua. This canyon is wider and deeper than the Grand Canyon of the Colorado River in Arizona.

Between these two mountain ranges lies the Central Plateau of Mexico. The northern part of the plateau is desert, similar to that of eastern New Mexico and western Texas; it is sparsely populated. The southern section has a moist climate and fertile soil, and is thus more heavily populated. Mexico City lies in the Valley of Mexico at the extreme southern end of the plateau, and on a clear day two permanently snow-covered volcanoes can be seen to the southeast.

The Mexican volcanoes run approximately along the 19th parallel, a line just south of Mexico City. The range is anchored on the east by El Pico de Orizaba, only 110 km (68.4 mi) from the Gulf of Mexico. These volcanic peaks mark the southern extension of North American physiographic features; some geographers regard this volcanic fracture zone as the southern termination of the North American continent. The range is known variously as the Cordillera de Anahuac, the Sierra Volcánica Transversal, or the Cordillera Neovolcánica.

Most Americans who visit central Mexico for the purpose of hiking and climbing concentrate on the three highest volcanoes—El Pico de Orizaba (5611 m; 18,410 ft), Popocatépetl or "Popo" (5465 m; 17,930 ft), and Iztaccíhuatl or "Ixta" (5230 m; 17,160 ft). Altitude is the only major difficulty usually encountered on these mountains. And herein lies their attraction: They allow mountaineers from the United States to climb to 5000 meters (16,400 ft) with a minimum of expense and time, thus allowing the climber to experience high altitude (though the total amount of time spent above 4300 meters [14,000 ft] is usually less than 24 hours). Equipment needed is the same as would be required for a climb of any of the major

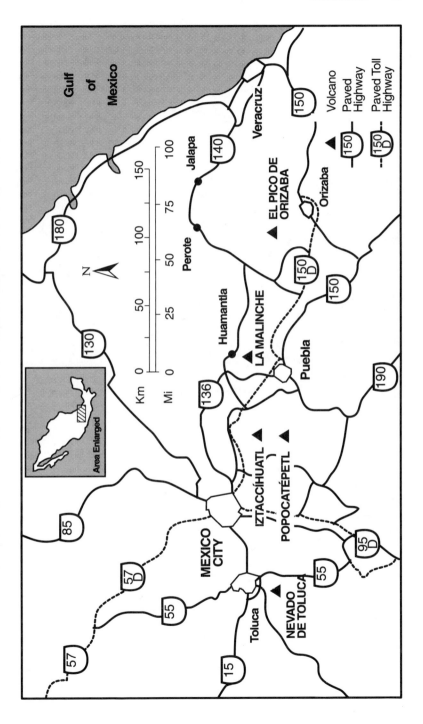

Ovens near Acatzingo (Photo by Rich Weber)

Cascade peaks or for a spring climb in the Sierra Nevada of California. Technical difficulties are minimal, though occasional snow and ice conditions demand the use of an ice axe, crampons, and rope.

Most mountaineers who climb Mexico's highest volcanoes climb them by way of their "tourist routes." While I do not belittle these great peaks, nor their "easy" routes (which have, on occasion, claimed the lives of climbers), I will point out their other routes and two of the other mountains in this area. This modest volume should not be considered a comprehensive guidebook to this range. Preference has been given to the higher, more prominent volcanoes.

The names of Mexico's volcanic mountains seem to be continually in dispute. Many Mexicans prefer to call them by their Aztec names, Citlaltépetl, for example, for the more modern El Pico de Orizaba. Others are in favor of the Spanish names. I prefer to use the Spanish names wherever possible and apologize to those who may be offended by this.

The altitudes of these mountains have also been disputed. Summit elevations have been taken from the 1987 edition of the Tactical Pilotage Chart J-24C, published by the Defense Mapping Agency Aerospace Center.

One of the principal difficulties encountered when visiting these mountains is the approach; sometimes the ascents seem trivial by comparison. Remote roads are often suitable only for trucks and other high-clearance vehicles; dry or wet weather often makes a considerable difference in their condition. Often the roads are unmarked. Please keep these points in mind while searching for a remote roadhead.

There are two unpleasant facets to exploring these mountains: the occasional lack of water and the litter surrounding the huts, routes, and summits of the higher peaks. The first problem can be taken care of by advance planning. The second is not so easy, for a party should pack out its own garbage, in addition to what is found on the mountain, and this latter amount can be considerable. With the exception of the huts at Tlamacas, Piedra Grande, and Malinche National Park, none of the other high-mountain structures has sanitary facilities, and the nearest open window may be used as a garbage chute. Visitors to these mountains would be doing those who follow a considerable service by removing their own rubbish and tidying up the huts as best they can.

Some people who climb these mountains appear to be merely "peak baggers." As soon as they are through with one volcano, they begin the ascent of another. Granted, the objective of most of these parties is to climb peaks, but the trip would undoubtedly be much more pleasant if more time were scheduled between climbs to explore the surrounding area and become acquainted with the people, Aztec ruins, restaurants, markets, and fiestas. Such a change in attitude could turn a "climbing trip" into a "climbing holiday," and considering the relative prices between the United States and Mexico, this prospect becomes quite attractive.

Iztaccíhuatl from Amecameca (Photo by Ray Smutek)

CHAPTER ONE

BACKGROUND

History

The Aztecs were one of the most civilized and powerful groups of Indians in the New World. For over 300 years they occupied the Valley of Mexico and surrounding areas, and from the capital city of Tenochtitlán (located near Mexico City), the Aztecs controlled a large empire that included most of central and southern Mexico. In addition to the prominent pyramids, they showed remarkable ingenuity in other areas of engineering. Tenochtitlán was built up from the shallow waters of Lake Texcoco; it was connected to the mainland on the north, west, and south by earthen causeways with movable drawbridges. Aqueducts carried fresh water into the city from springs in the nearby hills. The city had an estimated population of 100,000 when Cortés arrived.

Agriculture formed the basis of the Aztec economy, and although the soil was cultivated by means of simple digging sticks (they had no plows, beasts of burden, or iron tools), the farmers were able to produce enough food to supply not only their own needs, but also those of the workers and government officials in the city.

The Aztecs were famous warriors, with a highly developed military organization. When their armies went to war, they fought not only for political and economic advantage, but also for prisoners who were needed for large-scale human sacrifice.

The Aztecs' complex religious practices formed the basis of their culture. They named the surrounding high mountains after their gods and religious leaders. Citlaltépetl is Aztec for "The Star Mountain," and this name is connected with the legend that the body of Quetzalcoatl, the Plumed Serpent, was consumed by divine fire in the crater of the volcano. Quetzalcoatl, the Aztec god of learning and the priesthood, then took human form and sailed across the sea, bound to return to the land of the Aztecs in the future.

The Aztec name Popocatépetl translates as "The Smoking Mountain." According to legend, Popocatépetl, a warrior, was enamored of Iztaccíhuatl ("The Sleeping Woman"), daughter of the emperor. When Popocatépetl was returning from a victory in war to claim his beloved, his rivals sent word that he had been killed, and Iztaccíhuatl died of grief. Popocatépetl then built the great mountains that lie southeast of Tenochtitlán; on one he placed her body, and on the other he stands holding her funeral torch.

Before the Spanish conquest, Popocatépetl and Iztaccíhuatl were worshipped as deities. At festivals of the mountains, called Tepeylhuitl, images of Popocatépetl made of amaranth and corn were displayed. (Corn was a sacred plant to the Aztecs, and Mexicans still revere it today.) In one of the great temples of Tenochtitlán, a wooden idol of Iztaccíhuatl was a focal point.

There are no records of Aztec ascents of the high mountains, but it is possible that they climbed these peaks. On the northeast ridge of the Ventorrillo of Popocatépetl is a small enclosure of blocks and volcanic ash, the highest known structure of its kind in the region. It was probably built by the Aztecs or Toltecs (forerunners of the Aztecs) around 900 A.D. Several potsherds, as well as a broken piece of jade necklace and fragments of obsidian knives, have been found in this area. Similar relics have been found in the vicinity of Tlamacas.

The nature of the Aztec civilization could have allowed the opportunity to explore the upper reaches of the higher volcanoes. Perhaps on occasion a group of soldiers climbed to the summit of Citlaltépetl to scout the areas surrounding Veracruz, or some priests examined the crater of Popocatépetl to discover its hidden meanings, or a young man ventured onto the snow and ice of Iztaccíhuatl to satisfy his curiosity.

In 1518 the governor of Cuba became interested in the mainland west of

Church at Amecameca; Ixta in background (Photo by Rich Weber)

his island and assigned Hernando Cortés to command the small fleet and army he was sending to explore and look for treasure. Cortés at first explored and charted the coast of Yucatán, then moved north and landed at the present site of Veracruz on March 4, 1519. Indians along the coast had told him of the great wealth of the Aztecs, and after scuttling all of his ships, he set out in August 1519 with "... fifteen horsemen and three hundred foot [soldiers] as well accoutered for war as my resources and the short space of time would permit" to conquer a nation of six million.[1]

When Cortés and his men arrived in Cholula (near Puebla) in October 1519, Popocatépetl was erupting. The Indians assured him that no mortal would ever be capable of reaching the summit. To respond to this challenge and to satisfy his curiosity about the "secret of this smoke," Cortés sent Diego de Ordaz with nine Spanish soldiers and several Indians to attempt the ascent.

In a letter sent to Carlos V, King of Spain, dated October 30, 1520, Cortés stated the following:

Eight leagues from this city of Cholula there are two marvelously high mountains whose summits still at the end of August are covered with snow so that nothing else can be seen of them. From the higher of the two both by day and by night a great column of smoke comes forth and rises up into the clouds as straight as a staff, with such force that although a very violent wind continuously blows over the mountain range, yet it cannot change the direction of the column. Since I have ever been desirous of sending your Majesty a very particular account of everything that I met with in this land, I was eager to know the secret of this which seemed to me not a little marvelous and accordingly I sent ten men such as were well fitted for the expedition with certain natives to guide them to find out the secret of the smoke, where and how it arose. These men set out and made every effort to climb to the summit but without success on account of the thickness of the snow, the repeated windstorms in which ashes from the volcano were blown in their faces, and also the great severity of the temperature, but they reached very near the top, so near in fact that being there when the smoke began to rush out, they reported it did so with such noise and violence that the whole mountain seemed to fall down; thereupon they descended, bringing a quantity of snow and icicles for us to see, which seemed a novelty indeed, it being so hot everywhere in these parts according to the opinion of explorers up to now; especially since this land is said to be in the twentieth degree of

---

1. J. Bayard Morris, translator, *Hernando Cortés: Five Letters 1519–1526* (London: George Routledge & Sons, Ltd., 1928), p. 32.

The crater of Popocatépetl

latitude where great heat is always found... .

Two days after leaving Cholula we climbed the pass between the two mountains which I have already described, from which we could discern the province of Chalco belonging to Moctezuma... .

Early the next day I struck camp for a town two leagues further on called Amecameca, capital of the province of Chalco, which must number more than twenty thousand people, including the villages for some two miles around it. In this town we lodged in some excellent dwellings belonging to the chief ruler of the place.[2]

Historians of the conquest do not agree with Cortés about whether Diego de Ordaz reached the summit. During Cortés adventures, Ordaz became a bitter opponent, and in the grand tradition of all great adventurers, Cortés played down some of the exploits of his colleagues so attention would not be diverted from himself. Bernal Díaz, who accompanied Cortés during his conquest of Mexico and recorded everything encountered in great detail, gives credit to Ordaz and two companions for the first ascent. Lopez de

---

2. *Ibid.*, pp. 61–65.

Gomara gives similar credit in *Historia General de las Indias* (1552). An English translation of Gomara's work follows:

> *There is a hill eyght leagues from Chollola, called Popocatepec, which is to say, a hill of smoke, for manye tymes it casteth out smoke and fier. Cortez sente thither tenne Spanyards, with manye Iniians, to carry their vituall, and to guide them in the way. The ascending was very troublesome, and full of craggie rockes. They approached so nigh the toppe, that they heard such a terrible noyse which proceeded from thence, that they durst not goe unto it, for the ground dyd tremble and shake, and great quantitie of Ashes whyche disturbed the way: but yet two of them who seemed to me the most hardie, and desirous to see strange things, went up to the toppe, because thay would not returne with a valueless aunswere, and that they myghte not be accompted cowardes, leaving their fellowes behinde them, proceeded forwards. The Indians sayd, what meane these men: for as yet never mortallman tooke such a journey in hande.*
>
> *These two valieant fellowes passed through ye desert of Ashes, and at length came under a greate smoke verye thicke, and standing there a while, the darknesse vanished partly away, and then appeared the vulcan and concavetie, which was about halfe a league in compasse, out of whiche the ayre came rebounding, with a greate noyse, very shrill, and whistling, in short that the whole hil did tremble. It was to be compared unto an oven where glass is made. The smoke and heate was so greate, that could not abide it, and force were constreyned to returne by the way that they had ascended: but they were not gone farre, when the vulcan began to lash out flames of fier, ashes and imbers, yea and at last stones of burning fier: and if they had not chanced to finde a rocke, where under they shadowed themselves, undoubtedly they had there bin burned.*[3]

Gomara goes on to report that in 1540 Popocatépetl erupted again, apparently with much greater force than in 1519. It spread ash "... fifteen leagues distant, and burned the herbes in their gardens, their fieldes of corne, trees, and clothes that lay a drying."

Many alpine historians still question Ordaz's ascent; it seems doubtful that such a climb could be undertaken with the mountain erupting as it was. (However, in 1914 Lassen Peak in northern California violently erupted; and driven by the same curiosity as Diego de Ordaz and his men, a group of local gentlemen reached the summit to witness lakes of molten rock and pyroclastic bombs.) Moreover, Ordaz and his group had no ice axes or crampons. On

---

3. Francisco Lopez de Gomara, *The Pleasant Historie of the Conquest of Weast India* (London: Henry Bynneman, 1578), pp. 160–61.

the other hand, when a sulfur mining operation was established in the crater of Popocatépetl in the late nineteenth century, the miners climbed the peak daily wearing *huaraches* (sandals), the avant-garde mountaineering footwear of the day.

From reading all accounts of this ascent, I am inclined to believe that Ordaz reached the summit, or at least came very close to it. It appears that Ordaz climbed the mountain via the Ventorrillo route, which leads almost to the high point of the crater rim. In any event, Carlos V, the King of Spain, recognized the achievement of Ordaz as successful and allowed the family of Ordaz to commemorate the adventure by assuming a figure of the burning mountain on the family crest.

After Cortés finished his business in the vicinity of the volcanoes, he went to Tenochtitlán; after much difficulty (and several retreats and advances), he finally captured the city in 1521. After all of this activity, ammunition supplies became low, and a group of five conquistadors was dispatched to the crater of Popocatépetl to obtain sulfur, crucially needed for the manufacture of gunpowder. Although the following story of this mission seems incredible, it has been authenticated by every historian of the day.

Francisco Montaño and four others set out for Popocatépetl amid great acclaim. As they approached the base of the volcano, the crowd of sightseers swelled into the thousands; many built makeshift huts and lean-tos to await the outcome. Indians carried ropes, blankets, and bags to assist the soldiers in their duties. The party bivouacked partway up the volcano by digging a cave in the snow, but sulfur fumes and the cold temperatures forced them out and they stood there shivering in the dark, the stars obscured by clouds and smoke. While exercising to keep warm, one of the soldiers fell into a crevasse; fortunately he caught himself on a huge icicle and his companions extracted him after some time.

Shortly after they resumed their ascent, an eruption shook the mountain, and the party ran for shelter from the falling cannonades. One heated rock landed near them, and they crowded around it and warmed themselves. At this point one soldier became too exhausted to continue, and he waited there for the return of his fellow soldiers. As the rest of the party neared the crater, another explosion took place, this time with no convenient shelter.

Fortunately all remained unscathed, and the apprehensive group of four arrived at the crater rim. When the fumes, smoke, and steam cleared, they could see seething masses of lava beneath them. Occasionally the earth rumbled beneath their feet. The party cast lots to see which one of them would make the descent into the crater. The lot fell to Montaño, and his companions lowered him into the crater with a rope tied around his waist. The rope was probably a thin cord woven by Indians, perhaps some short ropes tied together. Montaño regarded the rope as an extremely slender support, which might at any moment break and send him into the hell that

Approaching El Pecho, Iztaccíhuatl

El Pico de Orizaba from the north; Piedra Grande to the far left

lay beneath him. Fortunately, the rope held, and Montaño's companions raised and lowered him seven times, with Montaño delivering a bag of sulfur each time. Juan de Larios then relieved the exhausted Montaño and made six trips into the crater. Montaño later stated that he was lowered into the crater a distance of 200 meters (657 ft), with mind and body oppressed by fumes and in danger of being hit by erupting substances. As a result of the efforts of these two men, 140 kilograms of sulfur were obtained. Deeming this sufficient, the men started their descent. After threading their way through several crevasses (and falling into a couple), slipping on icy surfaces, and colliding with sharp projections of loose-lying rocks, they approached their camp at the foot of Popocatépetl. The natives came forth with enthusiastic cheers and raised the adventurers onto their shoulders. The journey to Coyuhuacan (near Tlaxcala) was a triumphal march, and Cortés himself is said to have welcomed them with an embrace. In Cortés fourth letter to the king, dated October 15, 1524, he described their sulfur-mining operation and added, "… in the future this method of procuring it will be unnecessary; it is certainly dangerous and I am continually writing to Spain to provide us.…"[4]

The nineteenth century saw a resumption of explorations of the volcanoes. On September 28, 1803, Baron Alexander von Humboldt climbed Nevado de Toluca while examining the vertical distribution of plants and animals. Prior to visiting Mexico he and his companion, Aimé Bonpland, climbed to 5878 meters (19,286 ft) on Chimborazo in Ecuador. This set a new altitude record for Europeans (the previous record was set by Cortés soldiers on Popocatépetl). During his year-long stay in Mexico, von Humboldt also explored the lower reaches of El Pico de Orizaba, but did not reach its summit or crater rim. His chief concern while in Mexico was a geographic survey of the country, and his busy schedule precluded any other ascents of the high mountains.

In March 1847, 10,000 American soldiers under the command of Major General Winfield Scott landed near Veracruz. Their mission was to take Mexico City and ultimately gain a victory for the United States in the war with Mexico. Within six months the troops had taken the city, but it wasn't until February 1848 that the Treaty of Guadalupe Hidalgo was signed. During this interim period, many American soldiers explored the area surrounding Mexico City, Puebla, and Veracruz, cities they occupied at that time. Undoubtedly they were influenced by the writings of von Humboldt, who was becoming popular in the United States during this period. They made numerous excursions to the pyramids of Teotihuacan and Cholula. A party of Americans climbed Popocatépetl; and a group of American soldiers, led by Lt. William F. Raynolds, climbed El Pico de Orizaba during the occupation of the city of Orizaba.

Raynolds's party consisted of eight army officers, two naval officers, thirty-six enlisted men, and four native guides. A long pack train left the city of Orizaba and headed directly toward the volcano, spending the first night near the village of La Perla, on the southeastern flank of the mountain. After two more days the party camped at an approximate elevation of 12,000 feet. On May 10, 1848, twenty-four of the Americans made their summit attempt, climbing the route now known as El Perfil del Diablo. As would be expected at that time of the year, the party found loose volcanic sand covered with a light dusting of snow, at an angle of 33 degrees. After many hours of this tedious climbing, most of the party had dropped out, but five persevered and finally reached the relatively solid rock of the crater. They traversed left, encountering many false summits, until they reached the high point of the crater rim. A makeshift American flag was erected, and the party saluted it with three hearty cheers.

---

4. Morris, *op. cit.*, p. 275.

Popo from Paso de Cortés (Photo by Rich Weber)

On the Jamapa Glacier, El Pico de Orizaba

Raynolds was a member of the elite Topographical Engineers, and he wanted to measure the altitude of the peak. He had brought along a barometer in addition to a thermometer and an alcohol burner to determine the boiling point of water. He discovered that the bottle containing the alcohol was broken, but Raynolds wasn't one to miss out on a once-in-a-lifetime opportunity, so he tried to determine the boiling temperature of water at that altitude by burning whiskey! Unfortunately, this attempt failed. He then turned to his barometer and was shocked to see that the level of mercury was below the lowest point of the graduated scale. Raynolds's rough estimates led him to conclude that the summit was 17,907 feet in elevation. This figure is far different from the generally accepted modern figure of 18,410 feet, but prior to 1848 El Pico de Orizaba had been estimated to be 17,721 feet and 17,885 feet by von Humboldt and others. Raynolds believed that he stood on the highest point of North America. (Later in his career, Raynolds undertook a survey of Wyoming's Wind River Mountains and Teton Range in 1860. He named Union Pass in the Wind River Mountains during this exploration.)

Several residents of Mexico didn't believe that the Raynolds party had reached the summit of Orizaba. In 1851 a group of forty men set out to climb the peak; and as the journey progressed, several members of the party slowly gave up the attempt. At last a lone Frenchman, Alexander Doignon, reached the summit and found a tattered American flag with "1848" carved in its staff.

The first ascent of Iztaccíhuatl remained the great challenge. Some have given credit to a German named Sonneschmit for the first ascent in 1772; I am inclined to disbelieve this claim, considering the difficulties that parties encountered a hundred years later. Furthermore, if Sonneschmit was successful, then he climbed Iztaccíhuatl fourteen years before the first ascent of Mont Blanc.

All of the early attempts on Iztaccíhuatl originated in Amecameca, by way of either the Ayoloco or Ayolotepito glacier, both located on the western side of the mountain. During the late 1850s a geographic and geological survey was conducted in the vicinity of Iztaccíhuatl and Popocatépetl, and there were two or three attempts to reach the top of Iztaccíhuatl. The principal character behind these endeavors was Walker Fearn, the Secretary of the United States Legation in Mexico. Invariably these ascents were unsuccessful due to icy conditions and the lack of crampons and proper ice axes.

Years later a Briton attempted the peak without "rope or ice axe" because his Indian guide assured him they were unnecessary. Upon arrival at the snout of the glacier the guide "urged an immediate return, confessing that he had never gone further himself, and that he believed the mountain to be inaccessible." But they continued, and, "My guide (?), who followed me at a distance of about twenty yards, evidently thought the whole proceeding to be a good example of Englishman's idiocy." Unfortunately, "we found it impossible to proceed without danger and were reluctantly compelled to return, as a steep ice-slope about fifty yards wide effectively barred further progress to anyone unaided by an ice axe."[5]

In November of 1889, H. Remsen Whitehouse took time off from his diplomatic duties while serving as the British Minister to Mexico and set out for Iztaccíhuatl. He was accompanied by Baron von Zedwitz, the German Minister to Mexico. In two days they established themselves in a cave near the terminus of the Ayoloco Glacier on the western side of the mountain. At

---

5. A. R. Hamilton, "Ascents in Mexico," *The Alpine Journal*, Vol. XVIII (1896– 97), pp. 457–58.

four o'clock the next morning, they started up the glacier. Bare ice in the icefall presented some difficulty, but they made quick work of it by cutting steps with the wood axe they had brought along for such a situation. At nine o'clock that morning they arrived at the summit, only to discover a bottle with a calling card inside. James de Salis, a Swiss mountaineer who had attempted Iztaccíhuatl for over two years had reached the summit five days before Whitehouse and von Zedwitz.

In 1917 a recent graduate of Harvard University—Otis McAllister—started work with the Southern Pacific Railroad, which was involved with construction and maintenance of railways in Mexico. He was based in the Yaqui Indian region of northern Mexico, at Emplane, Sonora; and he spent his free time climbing many of the neighboring hills by himself. He had already had considerable mountaineering experience. Before attending Harvard, McAllister had made several explorations in the West—in the hills surrounding San Francisco and the mountains around Lake Tahoe. He joined one of the first Sierra Club High Trips in the Sierra Nevada in 1904, and had the privilege of meeting John Muir in the incomparable setting of Yosemite Valley. While attending Harvard, he visited Mount Mitchell in North Carolina and Mount Monadnock in New Hampshire. Over summer holidays he visited Europe and climbed the Piz Languard, the Faulhorn, the Rigi, and the Goerner Grat in the Alps. While in Scotland he climbed Ben Lomond, explored the Lake District in England, and visited Italy where he climbed Vesuvius. Before arriving in Mexico, McAllister climbed Mount Shasta and Mount Whitney in California.

After some time, McAllister was transferred to Mazatlán, but he eventually quit the railroad and moved to Mexico City where he became a school-teacher. Transportation was difficult in Mexico in the early 1920s, but McAllister managed to visit several of the mountains within the Distrito Federal. He began writing about his trips for a Mexico City newspaper, and gradually his students and other friends began to join him on these outings. In the grand tradition of other great mountaineering clubs, the Club de Exploraciones de México, A.C. (CEMAC)[6] was founded on the summit of Ajusco on March 26, 1922.

McAllister was the founder of the club and its driving force for over fifty years. Its organization was based on that of the Sierra Club. Even CEMAC's emblem has the same fundamental symbolism as the Sierra Club's emblem: a mountain, a tree, and a stream of water. Instead of Half Dome, the great Sequoia, and the Merced River, the Aztec symbols for a mountain, a tree, and a stream are used.

---

6. The "A.C." stands for Asociación Civil (Civil Association) and identifies the group as a nonprofit organization.

Approaching the summit of Popocatépetl

A review of the club's journal, *La Montaña* (*The Mountain*), first published in 1929, shows that the activities of the group have been similar to those of corresponding U.S. and Canadian clubs. In the early 1920s the club made ascents of the highest volcanoes and explored the valleys and Aztec ruins surrounding Mexico City. A change of emphasis occurred in the latter part of the decade, when parties began seeking out more difficult routes on the high volcanoes, and technical climbing gained more interest than snow slogs. In 1929 a party of twelve climbed La Amacuilecatl ("the feet" of Iztaccíhuatl), and another party explored the northern side of La Cabellera ("the hair"). The early part of the next decade saw a traverse of Iztaccíhuatl, ascents of the Ventorrillo of Popocatépetl and Las Torrecillas (Little Towers) on El Picó de Orizaba, and a descent into the crater of Popocatépetl. This last outing is significant in that it eventually led to the formation of a rock-climbing group for CEMAC.

After World War II, Mexican climbers entered the world mountaineering scene by completing ascents of Aconcagua, Mt. McKinley, the most severe climbs in the Alps, and the big walls of Yosemite Valley. On May 16, 1989, Ricardo Torres Nava became the first Mexican to climb Mt. Everest.

Geology

Volcanic activity in central Mexico began approximately 10 million years ago, during the late Miocene and Pliocene epochs. The volcanoes that were formed at that time were the forerunners of those that exist today. During that time Iztaccíhuatl was created, and the first of Popocatépetl's cones appeared, the remnant today being the Ventorrillo. Also during that period, the continents began to take their present shape and primitive mammals appeared.

The next major cycle of volcanic activity began early in the Pleistocene epoch, approximately 2.5 million years ago. The sites of activity generally moved south, and during this period El Pico de Orizaba and the present cones of Iztaccíhuatl and Popocatépetl were formed. Evidence seems to indicate that these original mountains were higher than they are today. Volcanic activity in the early Pleistocene epoch prevented permanent glaciers from forming on the high volcanoes, especially on Popocatépetl. By the end of the Illinoisan glacial period, eruptions diminished and allowed erosion to do its work, and ice fields developed that still remain on the mountains.

Since this period there have been numerous eruptions, especially on Popocatépetl, and with the exception of Paricutín, these eruptions have not changed the fundamental structure of the mountains. Today all of the volcanoes are dormant, with Popocatépetl spewing steam occasionally.

Glaciers have been receding slowly on the high volcanoes, but not as dramatically as some reports have indicated.[7] I suspect that the poor snow cover that was present on the volcanoes in the mid- to late 1980s was due to the same drought conditions that the rest of the western United States also experienced during this period. But after viewing photographs taken fifty years ago and comparing them with the glacial conditions that exist today, it is apparent that the amount of permanent snow and ice has decreased on these mountains.

---

7. John Rehmer, "Vanishing Ice on Mexico's Volcanoes," *Summit*, Vol. 34, No. 6 (Nov-Dec 1988), pp. 28–29. Also see Cameron Burns's letter, *Summit*, Vol. 35, No. 2 (Mar-Apr 1989), p. 35.

Popocatépetl from Amecameca (Photo by Rich Weber)

CHAPTER TWO

PREPARATIONS

Equipment

Some prefer to travel light, cutting their toothbrush in half and throwing out books like this one in the quest for ease of mobility. Others prefer to carry the whole catastrophe. In any case, while packing for your trip, keep the following points in mind.

Generally speaking, take along the same equipment you would carry for a climb of a glaciated Cascade peak or for a spring climb in the Sierra Nevada of California. The most common accidents in recent years on the high volcanoes have been involuntary glissades. Almost all of these accidents could have been prevented (or, at least, the damage would have been minimized) if the victims had been roped with other members of their party and had used ice axes instead of ski poles. In addition to a proper ice axe, good boots, crampons, and gaiters are needed. Weather conditions can be either hot or cold, so synthetic pile or wool trousers, sweaters, mittens, long underwear, a wool cap, and a scarf are desirable, in addition to dark glasses, broad-brimmed hat, and sunscreen for protection from high-altitude glare, which can be severe. It is smart to bring along raingear, and if a tent is carried it should be stormproof. A sleeping bag that is comfortable in below-freezing temperatures is necessary. Crevasses are prevalent on the volcanoes, and smart climbers will carry prusik slings, a rope, carabiners, and some type of snow anchors. It is assumed that visiting climbers know how to use all of this stuff.

Most Mexicans leave for the summit at four o'clock in the morning (regardless of the height of the camp), so a headlamp can be helpful. The interiors of the mountain huts are dark, and an ample supply of candles also would be handy. There aren't any foam pads or air mattresses in the high-mountain huts, so bring your own.

For many years, it was almost impossible to locate a supply of white gas in Mexico. This situation is now completely reversed, and white gas (*gasolina blanca*, *bencina*, or *nafta*) is now readily available almost everywhere, as long as you have your own container. I have had the best luck buying white gas in paint stores (*pinturas*), but it has also been found in hardware stores (*ferreterías*) and gas stations. This fuel is much more volatile than the stove and lantern fuel available in the United States; my white-gas backpacking stove roars best while burning Mexican white gas.

Prior to the second coming of white gas, many campers burned unleaded automobile fuel in their gasoline-powered camping appliances. The old unleaded fuel was known as Extra, and it was rarely available in the silver pump at a few PEMEX stations. The new unleaded fuel is Magna Sin, and it is now available in the green pumps at selected PEMEX stations throughout Mexico. Magna Sin would be a good backup choice if white gas cannot be obtained. In my experience, and speaking generally, the more high tech the stove, the more high tech the fuel needed; and the more low tech the stove, the more low tech the fuel needed. So, if you have a stove made of the latest materials and design (and it is pumped by means of a contraption that resembles a bicycle pump), you had better burn white gas in it, and if you have a stove made of brass and it operates on the same principle as a Molotov cocktail, Magna Sin may be used in a pinch.

Like white gas, butane cartridges also have mysteriously and miraculously appeared in the sporting-goods stores of Mexico. This includes all types of butane cartridges: blue ones, where the burner punctures the canister, and the screw-in, screw-out type. Steel propane cartridges are also available. A number of sporting-goods stores can be found in Mexico City along Calle Venustiano Carranza, between Avenidas Lázaro Cardenas and Gante. This block can be reached by taking Metro Line 1 to the Isabel La Católica station, walking north six blocks and then west two blocks. Metro Lines 2 and 3 also pass through this general area. Other sporting-goods stores in Mexico City, Puebla, and other major cities may also have these cartridges. I have found the easiest way to find these stores has been to look up *deportes* (sports) in the yellow pages of the local telephone directory, and then look for the word *campamento* (camp).

Kerosene is also available, but perhaps not as widely as it has been in the past. (It seems that most Mexican homes in rural areas now have propane or electrical appliances.) It is most frequently found in the open-air markets, but it may also be purchased from paint stores and a few PEMEX stations.

I hold a tent to be a grand nuisance while carrying it and an indispensable item once it is set up in the rain and snow. Although there are huts on all of the popular routes on the high volcanoes and with good timing you will have little use for a tent, on weekends and during Christmas holidays you can expect to find the huts full, so a tent would then fall under the category of "essentials." At other times it may be a heavy luxury.

Skis have been used occasionally on the volcanoes. Popo and Orizaba have been skied with both alpine and Nordic equipment. Before ski mountaineers start carrying their gear, however, they should remember how much effort is required to carry skis to an elevation of 5400 to 5700 meters (17,700 to 18,700 ft). Remember, high altitude affects judgment, and it is a long way to the bottom. Once when I was descending Popocatépetl, I saw someone who must have decided it would be easier to glissade. After a few seconds he realized the error in his judgment, but it was too late. The involuntary glissade was 700 meters (2,297 ft) long, and he got off lightly with a broken leg, fractured ankle, and numerous scars and contusions. (While this is not a skiing accident, I believe this incident demonstrates one of the central dangers of these mountains.) If you are an expert ski mountaineer, then the effort involved in carrying the gear to the summit and the risks of the descent will probably be worth the downhill run.

Other items that come in handy when speaking with locals and making friends are postcards of your hometown (especially pictures of buildings and other urban sights) and photographs of your family. Finally, if you don't enjoy Mexico as it is, then please don't go. If you do go, take a lot of friendship. Leave behind the "ugly American" traits of arrogance and self-proclaimed superiority.

Maps

Topographic maps (*cartas topográficas*) at a scale of 1:50,000 for all of Mexico are now available. The quality of these maps is equal to the topographic maps put out by the United States Geological Survey. But some errors are apparent on a few sheets. The most common one is that it seems as if every canyon bottom is marked by a perennial stream. In reality, most of these streams run only during the rainy season, usually from June through October. Also, it seems as if all of the terrain above 4000 meters (13,000 ft) has permanent snow cover on these maps; this is seldom the case.

I have had no luck ordering these maps from the United States and can only recommend purchasing them while in Mexico, but it seems as if the sheets covering the volcanoes are always out of stock. If the maps are in stock, take this as a good omen and buy them.

These maps are published by the Mexican government under the direction of INEGI, the Instituto Nacional de Estadística Geografía E Informática (which used to be Dirección General de Geografía, formerly CGNSI, which used to be DETENAL, and before that CETENAL). The main office for this agency is in the city of Aguascalientes, a long way from Mexico City. Fortunately, there are map outlets in Mexico City. If you are flying to the Mexico City airport, visit the outlet in the main terminal in booth 61. It is tiny, and the lone individual occupying this stall seems to have every single 1:50,000 topographic map of the country in stock, except for those sheets covering the volcanoes. But it is worth a try.

The next stop on the search for the elusive topographic maps is the main Mexico City office of INEGI, located at Balderas 71 in downtown Mexico City. Take Metro Line 1 to the Balderas station. The office is a short walk to the north, and it is on the west side of the street between Avenidas Morales and Ayuntamiento. Or take Metro Line 3, and get off at the Juárez station; the office is a short walk to the south.

El Pico de Orizaba is on the Coscomatepec sheet, catalog number E14B46, but the peak is in the southwest corner of this map. Tlachichuca is on the San Salvador El Seco sheet, catalog number E14B45. The southern approaches to El Pico de Orizaba are covered by Ciudad Serdán (E14B55) and Orizaba (E14B56).

Ixta and Popo are on the Huejotzingo sheet, catalog number E14B42. The western approaches to these peaks are on the Amecameca sheet, catalog number E14B41.

Malinche is on the Puebla sheet, catalog number E14B43, but the peak is in the extreme northeast corner of this map, and Tlaxcala, catalog number E14B33, is needed to climb Malinche from Campamento IMSS La Malintzin. The Huamantla (E14B34) and Tepatlaxco (E14B44) sheets cover the eastern side of the peak.

In the market, Amecameca (Photo by Rich Weber)

Nevado de Toluca is on the Volcán Nevado de Toluca sheet, catalog number E14A47.

The best roadmaps of Mexico are the *Carta Turística* (tourist map) series, published by INEGI. These maps are detailed, very accurate, full of information on places of interest, and very inexpensive. Six maps comprise this series, and the volcanoes are covered on the Centro and Sureste (Istmo) maps. The bad news is that these maps, too, are almost always out of stock. In fact, it is easier to locate roadmaps of Mexico in the United States than it is to find them in Mexico. And it is a good idea to travel to Mexico with at least one roadmap of Mexico (preferably several) in hand. Some American automobile clubs offer free maps to members. Also, Mexican insurance companies give away maps and road logs; be sure to ask for them.

Transportation

Tourism is a leading business in Mexico, so it is relatively easy to reach Mexico City from the United States, whether by plane, train, bus, or private automobile. Many who visit the volcanoes fly to Mexico City and then rent an automobile to approach the mountains. Renting a car has the advantage of flexibility; the only schedule to meet is your own. The disadvantage is the cost, for flying to Mexico City and then renting an automobile is the most expensive way to visit the volcanoes. But for those with limited time, this is the way to go.

The best advice I can give about renting a car in Mexico is to pretend that you are buying it. Have dents, scratches, missing hubcaps and antennas noted on the rental agreement. Is there a spare tire? Is it inflated? (Bring your own tire gauge!) Does the jack work? (Try it out at the rental agency, just in case.) Are the tires in good shape? Does the horn work? (You'll need it!) How about the windshield wipers, turn signals, brake lights, and headlamps? Check the oil and water, and then start the engine.

For those with a bit more time to spare, the trains that run to Mexico City offer the best bargain of all. These modern passenger trains, which take between 36 to 48 hours from the southern border of the United States to Mexico City, are relatively inexpensive.

Some travelers take the bus (*autobús*) to Mexico City, and most utilize this service in getting around from volcano to volcano. But bus routes and schedules change frequently, and it can be difficult getting accurate information. The first step is to find out which bus lines lead to your destination *and* which terminal or terminals serve each specific bus line. This information can be obtained most easily from hotels and tourist offices. Then, you must go to that terminal, locate the bus line, decipher the schedule, and purchase your ticket in person. If you're lucky, the bus will be leaving soon after you purchase your ticket. It seems that in most cases, however, one has to make two trips to the bus terminal: one to purchase tickets and another to board the bus. The most efficient way to purchase bus tickets in Mexico City may be to use the services of an agency, which can decipher the varying fares, routes, and schedules, buy tickets, and even have the tickets delivered to you, for a fee.

Autobuses de Oriente (more commonly known by its initials: A.D.O.) and Cristobal Colón (Christopher Columbus) provide regular and frequent bus service to Amecameca from Mexico City. A.D.O. also offers direct bus service between Mexico City and Cosmotepec, the city serving the eastern approach to El Pico de Orizaba.

Autobuses Unidos (more commonly known by its initials: A.U.) offers direct service from Mexico City to Tlachichuca, the jumping-off point for El Pico de Orizaba. This direct bus departs twice a day during the week and four times a day on Saturdays and Sundays.

Acosa offers direct, regular, and frequent service from Puebla to Ciudad Serdán and Tlachichuca. La Malinche is approached from Apizaco, and this city is served by bus from Mexico City by Autobuses Tlaxcala Apizaco Huamantla (ATAH).

Nevado de Toluca is near the city of Toluca, west of Mexico City. Flecha Roja (Red Arrow) and Autobuses de Occidente serve this city.

Transportation between the bus stop and the trailhead can be accomplished by taxi. Almost all small towns have at least one taxi available, and, failing that, it is very easy to hire a local driver to take you to the limit of the two-wheel-drive section of road. Considering the proximity of Popo and Ixta to Mexico City, it is interesting to note that some parties have hired a large taxi to take them from the Mexico City airport to the Vicente Guerrero Lodge on Popo and have made arrangements for the taxi to pick them up after their climb. This service is reliable, but it is only cost effective for a group of six to eight people.

Some drive their own vehicles to central Mexico. The trip takes three to five days from the U.S.–Mexico border and has the advantage of providing flexibility and a convenient place to store extra food and equipment while exploring the mountains. It also may be easier to reach the trailheads. But most American insurance policies are not honored south of the border. A Mexican auto insurance policy is not required to drive in Mexico, but it is highly recommended. If you are in an accident without insurance, you will most likely go to jail for quite a long time. A policy can be purchased easily in most border towns.

One of the problems most American drivers have faced over the years when driving their own cars to Mexico has been locating unleaded automobile gasoline. Unleaded fuel is now available all over Mexico in the form of Magna Sin, available from the green pumps at selected PEMEX stations. Regular leaded gas, known as Nova (a Mexican joke calls this fuel "No Va," in English, "It doesn't go") is in the blue pump, and diesel fuel is in the purple pump at all PEMEX stations, but only selected gas stations have Magna Sin. If Magna Sin were sold in the United States it would have an octane rating of 87, and Nova would have an octane rating of 80; PEMEX uses a different formula to compute octane ratings than that used in the United States. The supply of unleaded automobile gasoline will probably become universal throughout Mexico in the 1990s since Mexican federal law requires that all automobiles manufactured in that country after 1990 be equipped with catalytic converters, which must burn unleaded gasoline.

Whether you drive your own car to Mexico or rent one upon arrival, the following points on driving in the country may be useful. I don't drive at night in Mexico, and I don't recommend it. The roads are often in fair to poor shape, and cattle frequently wander onto the roads at night because the pavement is warmer than the fields. (Many buses have "cattle-catchers" built into their front grills.) There are also bicyclists, harvests, detours, motor-cycles with no lights, ice-cream carts, washed-out roads, washed-out bridges, soldiers, and other things on the road, and the point here is that everything you see during the day is still there at night, only you can't see it.

Sometimes a driver will signal that it is safe to pass by blinking the left turn signal. This is unnerving enough on blind curves and hills; it's even worse when you start to pass and the driver suddenly turns left onto some obscure side road. Be wary, too, of bridges that have room for only one vehicle at a time; right-of-way goes to the driver who flashes the headlights first. I always let the other driver go first.

Most of these dangers are absent on the toll (*cuota*) roads. On the other hand, these roads are expensive, and the tolls may be twice the cost of gasoline for the stretch covered. I have often found that the *libre* (free) roads, which run more or less parallel to the turnpikes, are just as fast, more scenic, and more interesting than their nearest competition.

Food and Water

When I travel to Mexico, I usually purchase most of my food upon arrival. *Supermercados* (supermarkets) carry the same fare (more or less) as their counterparts in the United States. Instant oatmeal seems to be unavail-able, but minute oats can be found, along with powdered soups, instant refried beans, oriental noodles, and small cans of meat and vegetables.

Many people from the United States who set out to climb the high volcanoes abstain from Mexican food in any way, shape, or form. This is regrettable, for one of the joys of visiting other areas is sampling the local foods, and I would encourage anyone visiting Mexico to try the offerings. To avoid illness, I follow this general rule: I don't put anything into my mouth that is questionable (and the local water is always questionable). It is a good idea to eat only those fruits and vegetables that can be peeled. First-class restaurants (usually found in tourist hotels) are reasonably safe, but with this security comes a higher price. The only general advice I can give is to look restaurants over; if you would feel comfortable eating food that comes from the kitchen, have your meal there.

For your safety, I repeat: Don't drink the water south of the border; if you swallow the wrong stuff, it can put you on your ear for a long time. If you're in a restaurant and ask for *agua purificado* (pure water), the waiter will probably bring you water from the tap, so it's better to drink beverages that don't contain water or ice cubes.

Don't plan to drink from mountain streams, either. While the best time of year to visit central Mexico is during the winter "dry" season, November through March, and this lack of rain and snow makes the climbing and hiking easier, it tends to dry up the high mountain streams. To add to the problem, volcanic rock and soil do an excellent job of absorbing water. Under these conditions, the possibility of locating a running stream above timberline is remote. A few streams may be running, but they may be polluted by improper disposal of garbage and human waste. Few of the huts have sanitary facilities, and garbage is sometimes deposited through the nearest open (or broken) window. It is usually best to carry an alternative supply of water.

I recommend purchasing bottled water in one of the larger cities, such as Mexico City, Puebla, or Tehuacan (this last city is famous for its mineral water). Many of the smaller towns aren't stocked with it (an exception is Amecameca). You will have to provide your own container or pay a deposit on a *garrafón*, a 20-liter (5-gallon) glass bottle. It may be better to purchase some lightweight plastic jugs from a hardware store to hold the water.

Health

I know as much about medicine as most politicians know about their constituents. But visitors may want to keep the following points in mind:
- Water found below timberline is always suspect.
- The most effective treatment of questionable water is boiling for 45 minutes.
- For chemical treatment, iodine appears to be more effective than chlorine.
- Don't add powdered fruit drinks to water treated with iodine; the iodine would rather attach itself to the carbohydrates in the drink mix than to the parasites, bacteria, and viruses in the water.

Even many Mexicans are not immune to the effects of their own water; immunity occurs as one's body gains resistance to the germs found in the local water and food, a process that can take a long time.

No immunizations are required for entry into Mexico, but many doctors recommend a gamma globulin shot to protect against hepatitis.

The main health concern on the volcanoes is the effects of high altitude. Different people have different reactions when exposed to altitude, and I continue to have different responses each time I go above 4600 meters (15,110 ft). This is undoubtedly due to several intervening variables for both myself and other people. On more than one occasion, I have seen Himalayan veterans flat on their backs in Mexico, while less experienced climbers in the same party continued to set a new personal altitude record with each bounding stride taken upward.

The major illnesses to watch out for include acute mountain sickness, high-altitude pulmonary edema, and cerebral edema.

Acute mountain sickness occurs after too rapid an ascent to 1500–1800 meters (5,000–6,000 ft). Symptoms include headache, dizziness, drowsiness, shortness of breath, nausea, and sometimes vomiting. The best cure is rest and descent to a lower elevation. At a lower altitude, the illness usually subsides fairly quickly.

High-altitude pulmonary edema is a serious, life-threatening medical emergency. It comes on rapidly, and has been known to cause death less than 40 hours after a rapid climb to 3000 meters (10,000 ft). The symptoms include a cough with bloody or foamy sputum, shortness of breath, general weakness, and a gurgling sound in the chest. If any of these symptoms appear, assume the worst and get the victim to a lower elevation as soon as possible. An authority on this illness, Dr. Charles S. Houston, has noted, "High altitude pulmonary edema may proceed rapidly to coma and death, or may improve with equal speed if the victim goes down only a few thousand feet after symptoms begin."[8] If the victim can't move under his or her own power, then *carry* him or her to a lower elevation. If oxygen is available, administer it.

Cerebral edema is not common (although I have seen one case of it) but is the most serious of the three discussed here. Symptoms include a severe headache, staggering, and hallucinations that could lead to coma and death. It rarely occurs below 4200 meters (13,780 ft). As with pulmonary edema, *carry the victim* (if necessary) to a lower elevation to save his or her life!

The best medicine is prevention, and there are some things that climbers can do to minimize their risks of illness and improve their performance.

Slow ascent. The mountaineer's dictum, "Climb high, sleep low," is the best method to prevent altitude sickness. The crucial factor is the *sleeping* altitude. Dr. Peter Hackett recommends, "Once above 3,000 meters, limit your net gain in altitude (your sleep altitude) to 300 meters per day (1,000 feet)."[9] In my experience, I have found the following rates to be a fair compromise for most people with limited vacation time on Mexico's volcanoes.

Day 1: Fly to Mexico City, no exertion, sleep there (2100 m; 7,000 ft).

Day 2: Travel to 3000 to 4000 meters (9,800–13,100 ft), no exertion, sleep there.

---

8. Charles S. Houston, M.D., "Altitude Illness—Recent Advances in Knowledge," *The American Alpine Journal*, Vol. 22, No. 1 (1979), p. 155.

9. Peter H. Hackett, M.D., *Mountain Sickness: Prevention, Recognition, and Treatment* (New York: American Alpine Club, 1980), p. 60.

Day 3: Day hike (that is, light packs) to 4500 to 4700 meters (14,800–15,400 ft), sleep at 3000 to 4000 meters (9,800–13,100 ft).

Day 4: Travel to 4000 to 4300 meters, no exertion, sleep there.

Day 5: Climb a high volcano!

Alternate climbing days with rest days for the remainder of this sample trip.

The minimum amount of time required to do the three high volcanoes with this schedule is ten days, or nine days if a late-night flight out of Mexico can be arranged on the last day.

Drink, drink, drink some more! Water, that is. In my experience, well-hydrated climbers acclimatize better than dehydrated climbers. Four liters or quarts per day is the minimum, and six liters or quarts per day is not too much. There is apparently no scientific evidence to support this, but the anecdotal evidence is there, both in my experience and that of professional researchers of altitude sickness. Think of water as a harmless recreational drug. I believe that it transforms my personality, making me more relaxed, more alert, and more attractive to members of the opposite sex.

Don't push yourself. Racing up a high volcano is a very good way to bring on mountain sickness. A slow, steady pace, such as the mountaineering rest step, will bring you to the summit much better and easier than the "dash and crash" that seems to be the norm. If your friends complain about your slow pace, find some new friends.

Don't drink alcohol. Even small amounts of alcohol seem to be detrimental to good acclimatization, in my experience. There is also some anecdotal evidence that alcohol may be a contributing factor to high-altitude cerebral edema. Besides, an overdose almost always results in some weird side effects!

Drugs. Many climbers take medication on the advice of their physicians to prevent or relieve the major symptoms of acute mountain sickness. My two drugs of choice are water and descent. If I have a headache at altitude, I drink a liter (quart) of water. The headache is usually gone by the time I finish the liter. If I still have a headache an hour later, I drink another liter, while descending.

Those going above timberline should be aware of hypothermia and prepare accordingly. Whether you are the type who can't differentiate between a butterfly closure and a Band-Aid, or one of those who has the capability of performing an appendectomy while standing in slings on the Big Wall, you should carry an adequate first-aid kit, with knowledge of how to use the contents.

Fortunately, the three major volcanoes have facilities for registration of climbs, and if your party doesn't return at the appointed hour people will be worried about you. It is always a good idea to register in advance and sign in on return. For Popocatépetl and Iztaccíhuatl, register at the Vicente

View of Popocatépetl from Ixta rest stop

Guerrero Lodge; on weekends the Socorro Alpino de México (Mountain Rescue Group of Mexico) is in attendance and gives free advice. For El Pico de Orizaba, register with the Reyes family in Tlachichuca. They keep climbing registers that go back many years, and visitors should not miss this opportunity to add their names to these historic documents.

In the event of an accident on Popocatépetl or Iztaccíhuatl, notify the staff of the Vicente Guerrero Lodge or the Ixta–Popo National Park rangers, if the Socorro Alpino de México is not immediately available. The best contact on El Pico de Orizaba is your four-wheel-drive driver. These individuals will get in contact with the appropriate agency, which may be the local rescue team, the local chapter of the Cruz Roja (Red Cross) or El Seguro Social (Social Security). (El Seguro Social has health clinics in most towns; they are marked on the 1:50,000-scale topographic maps with small black dots with white crosses.)

Try to leave someone with the injured climber, and try to send at least two people for help. Complete information is needed: How many are injured? Extent of injuries? Personnel on the scene? The exact location? Equipment available? Equipment and personnel needed? Don't expect anyone to speak English, so preferably one of the messengers should have a working command of Spanish or at least a dictionary.

The Mexican rescue groups are dependable and extremely skilled. But the rescue team may be a group of men from the local village with little or no mountain experience who generously offer their time and strength to help someone whom they have never met before. (At present, no helicopter rescue is available on the volcanoes.) Delays from three to five days are routine. Hopefully, all parties climbing the volcanoes will be self-sufficient in the event of an accident. When time is of the essence, and a human life is at stake, the resources of your own party (and other parties in the immediate vicinity) can make all the difference.

Guides and Clubs

There are alpine guides in Mexico, ready, willing, able, and eager to take you to a summit. Some of these guides can be reserved through travel agencies in Mexico City or Puebla. They offer complete services for a fee, even picking you up at the airport, bus station, or hotel in a four-wheel-drive truck, taking you on a mad dash (with meals and accommodations) to do *La Trilogía* (The Trilogy, that is, Popo, Ixta, and Orizaba), and returning you to the city. Other guides are stationed at the base of each volcano, and for a fee will lead you to the summit, leaving you with the chore of finding ground transportation and meals.

But there is another type of guide that is very useful when climbing Mexico's volcanoes. Far from being a professional alpine guide, this is usually someone who lives in the immediate vicinity and knows the shortest, most expeditious approach to the mountain. This type of guide is almost essential for the remote western and eastern approaches to El Pico de Orizaba, where there are many dead-end canyons, mazes of trails, and rare sources of running water. Once the guide and the client overcome their initial shyness, the guide will probably become a virtual fountain of information, proudly identifying landmarks, explaining local legends, customs, history, introducing you to his friends and family, keeping you out of trouble while giving you an in-depth introduction to another culture that few outsiders (this includes foreign tourists *and* other Mexicans) are allowed to see.

Before making arrangements with a guide, make an ironclad, but polite, agreement on the price (be generous) and services before the trip. The price is usually negotiable, and the fee may include room and board in the guide's home, ground transportation (either by jeep or truck, animal, or porters to carry your pack), and so on. As would be expected, the price goes up with the number of services desired by the client.

There are also many guide services in the United States that offer trips to the volcanoes. These companies usually advertise in climbing and outdoor magazines.

There must be thousands of mountaineering clubs in Mexico. The oldest and best known is the Club de Exploraciones de México (Exploration Club of Mexico). This organization was founded on the summit of the volcano Ajusco (south of Mexico City) in 1922. It is based in Mexico City and now has chapters in all of the major cities of Mexico. The Club Citlaltépetl is based in Puebla and serves as the primary authority on El Pico de Orizaba, or, as this club prefers to call it, El Volcán de San Andrés. The Sección Alta Montaña of the Cruz Roja and the Socorro Alpino de México specialize in mountain rescue, and their members have made ascents of some of the great mountains of the world. Dios y Montaña consists of members of the clergy and laymen who actively visit the mountains; they are responsible for the numerous crosses, memorials, and shrines that can be seen on the prominent routes on the volcanoes. Private industry and the public-service agencies (the Metro system of Mexico City has a very active climbing club), youth groups, churches, and boy scouts also make up a sizable portion of the Mexican mountaineering community.

Perhaps the most interesting Mexican mountaineering club is El Grupo de Los Cien (The Group of One Hundred). This organization was founded in 1950 with the purpose of constructing huts on the high volcanoes of Mexico for the use of all climbers. The founders were 100 individuals who each contributed 100 pesos (a considerable sum of money in the 1950s) to the club. Thus far, the club has built a total of eighteen huts, raising their own funds and building the structures with their own labor, and eleven of these are still in working condition. Their construction program has continued, and contributions may be sent to either of the following addresses: Señor Roberto H. du Tilly, Presidente, El Grupo de Los Cien, A.C., Sierra Nevada 635, Lomas de Chapultepec, 11000 México, D.F., or Señor Daniel Méndez Franco, Secretario, El Grupo de Los Cien, A.C., Medellin 86, Colonia Roma, 06700 México, D.F.

Bandits

I have never encountered a bandit in Mexico. But this appears to be the number-one fear of Americans visiting Mexico. The Club de Exploraciones de México offers the following rules "to maintain the security of the group":

- Have no less than four people in the group.
- The group stays together, no exceptions.
- Carry your camera in your knapsack, and take it out only when you are using it.
- Avoid attracting attention to yourself or to the group.
- No alcoholic beverages or firearms are allowed.

It may be comforting for uneasy people to note that most of the "professional thieves" (this includes mercenaries, pickpockets, assassins, bank robbers, and international jewel thieves) hang out in the big cities and resort towns of Mexico. But there is still the possibility that the "amateurs" (this includes the local population and foreigners, like you) will stroll by your hut or campsite and help themselves to whatever goodies happen to be lying around.

The best general advice I can give you to avoid trouble is this: Don't do anything dumb. Carrying a camera into a crowded market is dumb. Leaving your possessions unattended, even for a second, is dumb. Camping near a populated area without a guard is dumb. Attracting attention to yourself (by appearance or actions) is dumb. Making enemies instead of friends is dumb. Think about the security of your own party and those who might follow. And don't do anything dumb!

Don't be overly concerned about getting ripped off. It is an excellent way to spoil what would otherwise be a good trip. Compared to most countries of the world (and in some respects, the United States) Mexico is a very safe place to be, especially in the countryside and out of the cities. Still it is always a good idea to be cautious no matter where you are, either in the city or the country, or at home or abroad.

Climate, Weather, and Snow Conditions

The rainy season in Mexico occurs during the summer months, and this makes hikes and climbs in the mountains unpleasant and, to a certain extent, hazardous. Avalanches have been known to occur during this period of wet weather and warm temperatures. Whiteouts are also prevalent during this period, along with thunderstorms. The volcanoes can be climbed year-round, but the odds for success lie in the dry winter, the period from November to March. All of the above-mentioned conditions can also occur during this period, but in winter they occur much less frequently.

Anyone headed above the snowline should be prepared for the possibility of storms, whiteouts, and icy snow conditions. The mean freezing level is at 4200 meters (approximately 14,000 ft), and timberline is at 4000 meters (13,000 ft). Lenticular cloud caps can be seen over the volcanoes on occasion, and the prudent mountaineer will take compass bearings on prominent landmarks to ensure a quick and safe return.

I saw Popocatépetl covered with 30 centimeters of powder snow one year, and another year it was a continuous sheet of ice. These conditions vary with the month, the amount of precipitation versus the amount of sunshine, freeze-thaw conditions, and the general weather for the given year. The southern sides of the high peaks are often completely bare of snow, and climbing volcanic cinders and sand is unpleasant at higher elevations. Popo, Ixta, and Orizaba are the only peaks in Mexico with permanent snow.

When is the best time to visit the volcanoes? Most of the snow falls during the summer months. So one can expect to find good snow conditions (and running water) in late October, November, and early December, followed by increasingly icy (and dry) conditions as the dry season progresses into January, February, and March. In my experience, I have found the best snow conditions in October, but the weather is more unstable at this time than in November. On one trip to the volcanoes in early October, we had excellent snow conditions, but clouds obscured the view from the summits on more than one occasion, the jeep driver on Orizaba was unable to drive to Piedra Grande due to recent snowfall, and a major tropical storm passed through Mexico with severe floods in the mountains and along the Gulf of Mexico. Despite these miseries, we still had fun!

It seems that most climbers visit the volcanoes during Christmas. This is a long holiday period in Mexico, lasting from December 16 through 25. Celebrations begin again on December 31 (New Year's Eve and Mexico's Thanksgiving) and continue through January 6 (Three Kings Days). The disadvantage to this period is the crowds; it seems as if everyone in the country and most everyone from overseas is on vacation on Mexico's volcanoes. The huts are almost always full, and the guides, jeep drivers, and others who serve climbers would rather be celebrating the holidays with their families than entertaining climbers. I discourage climbers from visiting the volcanoes during Christmas.

Human Impact

If you haven't figured it out yet, these mountains see a lot of traffic. This should come as no surprise, for one of the world's largest cities is nearby and the number of foreign visitors increases every year. Mexico's bureaucracy has not yet reached such an advanced state where the number of climbers is controlled by a quota system. Visitors can help maintain the aesthetic beauty of these mountains by following a few suggestions.

When camping below 4000 meters (13,000 ft), be careful with fire. The grass can be dry, and once ignited it could burn for several kilometers.

The numerous huts on these mountains confine the human impact to small areas. These volcanoes are able to withstand a much greater human impact because of these shelters. Instead of 100 different permanent camping scars, there are only a few messy spots. There is still some litter around these huts and along the climbing routes, but not as much as there has been in past years. I find it very heartening that Mexican climbers have started to clean their own mountains. I once saw a local climber packing a load of trash down Iztaccíhuatl. He turned to me and said, "You *norteamericanos* respect our mountains more than we do." Setting an example works: Pack out your own litter and that of your predecessors.

On the road to Piedra Grande

Most of the streams above 4000 meters (13,000 ft) are reasonably pure and probably fit to drink. To ensure that they remain that way, bury human waste in a shallow hole at least 90 meters (300 ft) away from any water supply, hut, or other campsite. Don't wash dishes in any streams. Don't pollute the streams with soap, detergent, or other substances.

Don't deface trees, rocks, or other natural features. Leave plants, animal life, and archaeological sites for others to enjoy.

Please, don't destroy the mountain huts. They have been built by volunteers, with their own labor and funds, for the use of all climbers. Shut doors and windows before leaving. Once someone left the door to a hut open, and the next morning there was a layer of ice on the floor; I had to put on crampons just to cook breakfast.

Minor Details

Most banks and businesses are closed on the following holidays: January 1, January 6, February 5, February 24, March 18, March 21, May 1, May 5,

May 10, September 16, October 12, November 1, November 2, November 20, December 24, December 25, and December 31.

Not all banks handle foreign-exchange transactions. Those that do are located in the big cities, such as Mexico City or Puebla, and exchanges are made only between the hours of 10:30 A.M. and 12:30 P.M.

Check with your long-distance service about how to place calls from or to the United States and Mexico. The codes you probably will need are an international access code, a country code, a city code, and a local phone number. In most places in Mexico, one can call the United States and Canada by dialing 95 + area code + telephone number, but be forewarned: This seldom works, is really expensive, and you will be charged even if the call doesn't go through! Long-distance telephone service within Mexico is somewhat more dependable; you can try it by dialing 91 + the city code + telephone number.

Getting Out of Mexico City

Mexico City is the largest city in the world. Aside from its human population, it grew at the rate of 400 new cars *per day* in the 1970s. In the downtown area, the streets are like four-lane parking lots during most of the day and early evening hours. The names of streets seem to change with every block, and one-way streets seem to change direction with every other block. It may take twenty minutes to get through a major intersection. It has taken me six hours to drive from Veracruz to Mexico City (432 km, 268 mi), and another two hours to drive the 10 kilometers (6.2 mi) from the outskirts of the city to my home in the city. It would appear that the hardest part of climbing the volcanoes is navigating through Mexico City.

The government of Mexico City has initiated a program to reduce traffic and air pollution. Vehicles with license plate numbers ending with a 5 or a 6 cannot be driven on Mondays. On Tuesdays, the prohibited numbers are 7 and 8, Wednesdays 3 and 4, Thursdays 1 and 2, Fridays 9 and 0. All vehicles may be driven on Saturdays and Sundays, and these restrictions do not apply between the hours of 10:00 P.M. and 5:00 A.M.

It must be stressed that these restrictions apply to all privately owned cars and trucks, including vehicles with plates from other countries and Mexican rental cars. Be advised that a violation is much more severe (a large fine and vehicle impoundment) than the petty harassments tourists may suffer from the Mexico City transit police.

At present, there are few ways to avoid Mexico City. The best option at this time may be to fly into Veracruz and approach the volcanoes from there. There is also a similar size airport near Tehuacan, but it does not have as many scheduled flights as the Veracruz airport does.

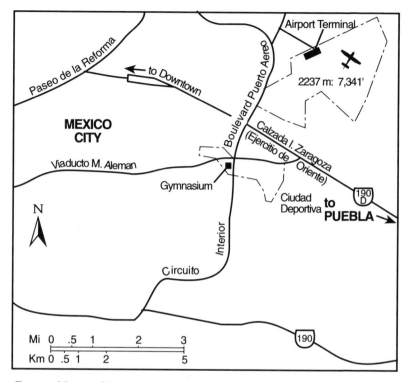

Eastern Mexico City

But, as in Rome, all roads seem to lead to Mexico City. After purchasing a map of the city at the Mexico City airport (2237 m; 7,341 ft), strap yourself into your rental automobile and prepare to face the masses. Those headed for Iztaccíhuatl, Popocatépetl, El Pico de Orizaba, and La Malinche want to head southeast, toward Puebla. The first step is to head south on Boulevard Puerto Aereo (which may be shortened to "Blvrd. Pto. Aereo"); a long, circuitous ramp leads to the correct street and direction. Continue south on Blvrd. Puerto Aereo, passing over Avenida Hangares to the next major cross street: Calzada General Ignacio Zaragoza (shortened to I. Zaragoza and also known as Ejercitio de Oriente or Highway 190-D). The approach to this street is easy to miss; there is only one small sign, "I. Zaragoza," on the right side of Blvrd. Puerto Aereo that identifies the correct place to leave Blvrd. Puerto Aereo for Calzada I. Zaragoza. Those who leave Blvrd. Puerto Aereo at the correct location will drop down below, and soon turn left under Blvrd. Puerto Aereo at a traffic light and will be on the correct highway leading southeast out of Mexico City: Highway 190-D. (A lot of transit police

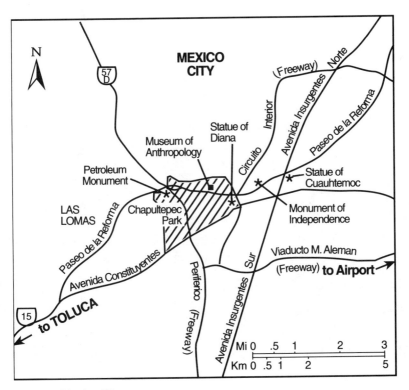

Western Mexico City

officers loiter at this corner and fine tourists in rental cars.) If you miss this street and head too far south, you will pass Ciudad Deportiva, a huge gymnasium used during the 1968 Olympic Games.

If your destination is Nevado de Toluca, take Highway 15 west. From downtown Mexico City, take the Paseo de la Reforma west. After passing through Chapultepec Park, you will pass a monument commemorating the nationalization of the oil companies, which occurred in 1938. Shortly after this, you will drive through the Las Lomas area of the city, with such street names as Chimborazo, Aconcagua, Sierra Negra, Torrecillas, Cotopaxi, Monte Blanco, Alpes, and Himalaya. Stay on the Reforma until it becomes the Carreterra a Toluca, also known as Highway 15.

Popocatépetl from Iztaccíhuatl

CHAPTER THREE

POPOCATÉPETL AND IZTACCÍHUATL

Most foreign climbers visit Popocatépetl and Iztaccíhuatl before other Mexican volcanoes, and the Popo–Ixta National Park is a popular destination for families on day outings from Mexico City. The mountains are about 80 kilometers (50 mi) from the Mexican capital, and it is not unusual for local *alpinistas* to climb either mountain in a day outing from the city. What was unusual, however, were two American climbers who took a flight on a Friday night to Mexico City, hired a taxi at the airport to drive them to Tlamacas, and climbed Popo on Saturday. On Sunday, the taxi took them to La Joya, they climbed Ixta, and the cab returned them to the airport in time for their flight home. I admire the accomplishment of these two women, but I can't help but think that they should reexamine their priorities.

To get to Popo–Ixta National Park from Mexico City, take Highway 190-

D, heading southeast toward Puebla. At the first toll station, pull over to the far right-hand booth (the booths on the left side lead to Puebla). The booth on the far right-hand side has a sign over it reading "Cuautla" (a nearby town). Pay the toll and then drive parallel to the highway for several kilometers. Leave the road at Highway 115-South. After passing through Chalco and Tlalmanalco, you'll reach Amecameca. Food, bottled water, and other last-minute purchases can be made in Amecameca (2460 m; 8,070 ft). Those taking the bus can locate a taxi at the plaza to take them to the lodge at Tlamacas.

If driving from Acapulco, Taxco, or Cuernavaca, it is much easier to drive directly to Amecameca, rather than through Mexico City. Take Highway 160-East from Cuernavaca to its junction with Highway 115, at a point just north of Cuautla and south of Amecameca; then, head north on Highway 115 to Amecameca.

From Amecameca, drive south on Highway 115. After 1 kilometer (0.6 mi), there is an intersection with signs pointing the way to Popo–Ixta National Park. Go east up this steep and winding road for 24 kilometers (14.9

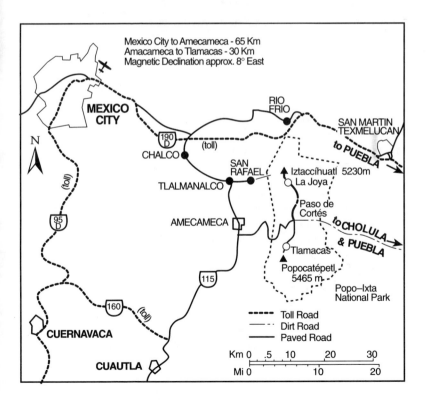

Vicente Guerrero Lodge, Tlamacas, with Popo in background (Photo by Ray Smutek)

mi) to Paso de Cortés at 3680 meters (12,073 ft). This is the low point between Popo and Ixta. Cortés crossed this pass in 1519, and from here he saw the city of Tenochtitlán. A small monument commemorates this event. There is a visitors center near the top of this pass.

It is possible to reach the Paso de Cortés directly from Puebla. A dirt road leads to the pass from Cholula, a town west of Puebla. This road consists of more sand than dirt, and it is only passable in good weather.

From Paso de Cortés, a dirt road leads north to the La Joya roadhead for Ixta. If bound for Popocatépetl, follow the paved road that leads south from the pass. There is a camping area about 2 kilometers (1.2 mi) up the road from the pass, but there are no facilities except for a few fireplaces; water and toilets are absent.

Another kilometer (0.6 mi) up the road leads to Tlamacas (3950 m; 12,960 ft) where there are two lodges. The newer one is the magnificent Vicente Guerrero Lodge, completed in late 1978. I believe that "magnificent" is a just word, for the closest thing I have seen that would resemble it in the United States would be Timberline Lodge on Mount Hood. Beds with blankets and sheets are available, along with flush toilets and hot showers for a nominal fee; the rate is extremely low by United States standards. Each bunk has its own locker; bring your own padlock. Tap water in the lodge is reported to be safe to drink, but should be purified anyway. There is a cafeteria on the premises, as well as a bar and two lounges with fireplaces. The staff of the lodge will watch your gear for you while you are away climbing. Adjacent to the lodge is a building that houses the Socorro Alpino de México. Members usually are in attendance over weekends, and it would be prudent to register your climb with them.

The other lodge is north of, and just below, the Vicente Guerrero Lodge. Here the accommodations are rather spartan (compared to the new lodge), with bunk rooms and a somewhat dirty and sooty main room. This lodge is almost always closed during the week, and may be open over the weekend. In the latter case, both lodges will probably be packed to capacity.

Don't leave any valuables overnight in an automobile, even a locked one, in either of the lodges' parking areas. This includes items left in the trunk. Either have a non-climber guard equipment while the rest of the party is away, or carry it inside the lodge and have the staff watch it. Never leave anything unattended inside either lodge.

Climbing Routes on Popocatépetl

All of the climbing routes on Popo are on the 1:50,000 Huejotzingo map, catalog number E14B42.

Lounge in the Vicente Guerrero Lodge

Popo from Iztaccihuatl; "The Feet" can be seen to the left

Iztaccíhuatl and Popocatépetl from the north

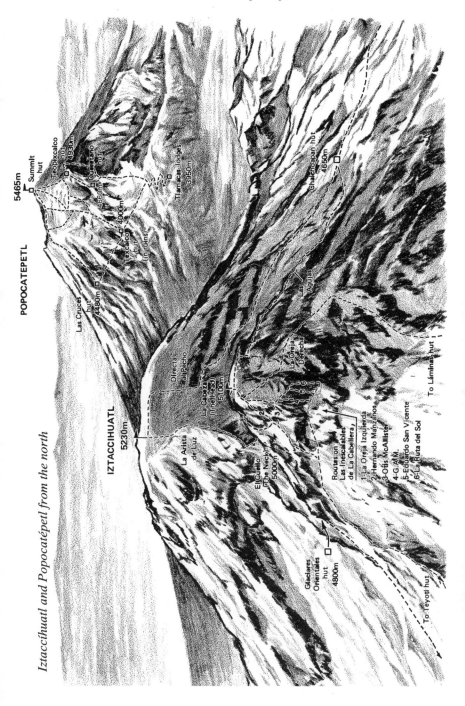

POPOCATEPETL

5465m
Summit
hut

Teopixcalco
hut 4950m

Queretano
hut

4660m

Tlamacas lodge
3950m

Chalchoapan hut
4660m

Texcalco
hut
[in ruins]

4000m

Las Cruces
hut
4480m

IZTACCIHUATL

5230m

Directa
al Pecho

La Cabeza (The Head)
5100m

La Arista
de Luz

El Cuello (The Neck)
5000m

Las Agujas

La Oreja
Derecha

Routes on
Las Inescalables
de La Cabellera

1-La Oreja Izquierda
2-Hernando Mahzános
3-Otis McAllister
4-G.A.M.
5-Eduardo San Vicente
6-La Ruta del Sol

Glaciares
Orientales
hut
4800m

To Teyotl hut

To Láminas hut

A dog atop Las Cruces route, Popocatépetl

Las Cruces (The Crosses)

This is the most popular route on the mountain, having been climbed by persons wearing *huaraches* and by burros (the latter's footwear remains unknown). I once climbed the peak and was followed by a dog all the way to the summit. On the other hand, once I saw a climber who thought it would be easier to descend the route by glissading. He lost control and slid quite a distance before the scree at the base of the peak stopped him. Whiteouts and cloudcaps are common, so Popo demands respect, even in the best of conditions.

From Tlamacas, follow a well-defined trail that leads east along the base of the volcano. This trail could be called a road, and it is easy to follow before sunrise. The trail forks before reaching Las Cruces; take the steep, right-hand, wide path (not the left-hand "road"). The trail ends at the site of the ruins of the Las Cruces hut (4480 m; 14,698 ft), 500 meters (1,640 ft) and 3 kilometers (1.9 mi) from Tlamacas. This hike takes about two hours.

From Las Cruces, the directions to the summit are simple: Climb straight up the 30-degree slope until the crater rim is reached. One usually has to negotiate a band of scree above the ruins of the hut until axes and crampons become useful. Upon arrival at the crater rim, turn right, and after 45 minutes or so, the shelter that marks the Pico Mayor (the true summit) comes into view. The ascent should take from five to eight hours from Tlamacas.

The central attraction of Popocatépetl is the crater. The crater rim is elliptical, with the long axis measuring 870 meters (2,850 ft) and the short axis measuring 620 meters (2,035 ft); the circumference is 2.3 kilometers (1.4 mi). The high point is on the west side of the crater, and from there the crater measures 480 meters (1,575 ft) deep. The walls of the crater are nearly vertical, and there are several small lava domes and a small lake on the crater floor. Several fumaroles dot the floor, wall, and rim of the crater, and often their fumes make an extended stay on the summit uncomfortable (some climbers have passed out from inhaling too much gas!). In 1921, a small spatter cone formed on the floor of the crater; this was the last significant volcanic activity. But some local climbers have indicated to me that the volcano seems to be warming up. At one time there was a sulfur-mining operation in the crater, with the miners climbing the peak daily to be lowered from the rim by means of a capstan. A tragic accident brought this operation to a quick end, however.

El Glaciar Norte (The North Glacier)

This route has also been called Ruta Central (Central Route). On the north side of Popo a large group of crevasses can be seen. This route follows the snow and ice slope to the left of these crevasses. About 2.5 kilometers (1.6 mi) from Tlamacas along the trail leading to Las Cruces lie the ruins of the Texcalco hut. From the hut, climb over some interminable scree slopes to the snout of the glacier, a narrow tongue of ice to the right of a wide, curving rock cliff (locally known as La Herradura, The Horseshoe). Above the snout, the slope angles 35 to 40 degrees. Once above the level of the crevasses, the crater rim can be reached by any number of routes, but the summit is up and to the right. Ropes and prusik slings are recommended due to the possibility of hidden crevasses.

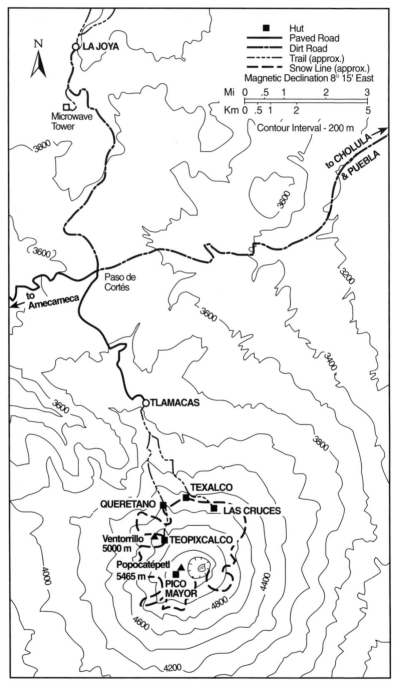

Popocatépetl

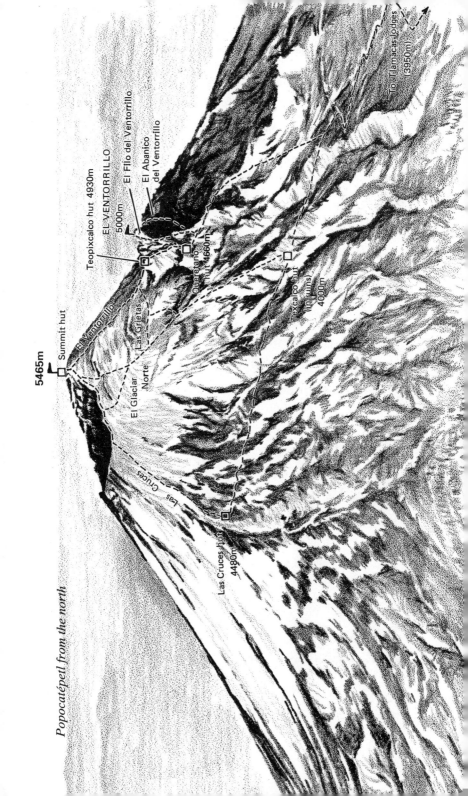

Popocatépetl from the north

5465m
Summit hut

El Ventorrillo

El Glaciar
Norte

Las Grietas

Las Cruces

Teopixcalco hut 4930m

EL VENTORRILLO
5000m

El Filo del Ventorrillo

El Abanico
del Ventorrillo

Queretano
hut 4660m

Texcalco hut
(in ruins)
4000m

Las Cruces hut
4480m

To Tlamacas lodges
(3950m)

Las Grietas (The Crevasses)

This illogical route leads directly to the crevasses mentioned for the Glaciar Norte (North Glacier) route, but it features the steepest ice climbing on the mountain. Follow the Glaciar Norte route to the vicinity of the snout of the glacier. Traverse right, around a small, curved ridge to the next glacier snout to the west. (Some may be tempted to approach this glacier directly from the canyon beneath it; this approach is not recommended.) Surmount the snout of the glacier; this is the crux of the climb and the easiest route depends on the snow and ice conditions. Above the snout, climb straight up to the huge crevasses. From here, either traverse left (east) to the Las Cruces or Glaciar Norte routes, or traverse right (west) to the Ventorrillo route. If conditions allow it, zigzag through the crevasses and climb directly to the crater rim. It almost goes without saying that crevasse rescue equipment should be carried.

A couple of variations have been done. The easiest approaches the crevasses from the Glaciar Norte route. The harder variation approaches the crevasses by leaving the Ventorrillo route somewhere between the Queretano and Teopixcalco huts.

El Ventorrillo

This is the preferred route for climbers of intermediate experience. It is the most direct route from Tlamacas, and it is located in a spectacular and

El Glaciar Norte, Popo (Photo by Ray Smutek)

Climbing El Ventorrillo route, Popocatépetl

Descending the crater rim to the Las Cruces route, Popocatépetl

Approaching the Queretano hut on Popocatépetl

exhilarating setting. There are two huts on the route, and even though they are not really needed due to the proximity of the roadhead, they offer the opportunity to sleep high on the mountain with tremendous views from their balconies. For those who are more than peak baggers, this is the way to go. (It would appear that this is the route that the conquistadors followed.)

From Tlamacas, take the Las Cruces trail until a smaller trail forks to the right at approximately 4100 meters (13,450 ft). This trail leads to the northeast ridge of the Ventorrillo. From the ridge, the trail leads to the Queretano hut at 4660 meters (15,288 ft). This hut is located on a spectacular overhanging cliff that overlooks the canyon that separates the Ventorrillo from the glaciers of Popocatépetl; it would be an interesting and comfortable place to spend the night. Above the cliff hut the route remains on the canyon side of the upper northeast ridge of the Ventorrillo. Avoid dropping into the canyon; it is much better to stay high on the shelf between the cliffs of the Ventorrillo and the cliffs of the canyon. The Teopixcalco hut is located at the saddle at 4930 meters (16,175 ft). (Those wishing to climb the Ventorrillo will find it a short scramble from the saddle.) Rope up at the saddle, and climb directly to the main peak of Popocatépetl. The slope averages 35 degrees, with occasional stretches at 40 degrees. The angle lessens to the left,

Popocatépetl from Paso de Cortés (Photo by Rich Weber)

El Ventorrillo from the north

5000m

El Abanico
del Ventorrillo

El Filo
del Ventorrillo

Queretano
hut

4660m

To Tlamacas

Climbing El Ventorrillo route, Popocatépetl

The Teopixcalco hut, Popocatépetl, with Ixta in background

The Queretano hut on Popocatépetl

On El Ventorrillo route, Popocatépetl

Popocatépetl's shadow at sunrise

High on El Ventorrillo route, Popocatépetl

but more crevasses are encountered. Farther to the right there are fewer crevasses, but the angle increases considerably. Between five to seven hours after leaving Tlamacas, the smell of sulfur will become apparent, and the summit should be nearby.

El Filo del Ventorrillo (The Ridge of the Ventorrillo)

The upper northeast ridge of the Ventorrillo is marked by a deep gap. Take the trail that leads to the Ventorrillo route and continue up the ridge leading to the summit of the Ventorrillo. The gap is negotiated by means of interesting down-climbing and rappels. Regain the ridge on the other side of the gap and follow it to the summit. Helmets, ropes, and hardware should be taken on the class-4 to class-5 climb.

El Abanico del Ventorrillo (The Palisade of the Ventorrillo)

This is the most difficult rock climb on Popo, consisting of the unholy trinity of mixed climbing (that is, all styles of mixed climbing: free, aid, and ice). It is best done in the middle of the winter, so that most of the loose rock is frozen into place. Approach the base of this face by means of the trail for the Ventorrillo route. Before reaching the northeast ridge, several rock outcroppings can be seen on the ridge leading north. Hike up to the top of these rocks and traverse right, atop the higher of the two prominent rock bands leading across the slope beneath the cliff. Head for a prominent break in the first cliff band above the slope. This is overcome by a short pitch (10 m; 30 ft) of free climbing and ends on a ledge atop the first cliff band. Move 3 meters to the right to a large, loose block, and climb over this block and continue up to some small ledges. Climb up and left from these ledges, and then continue straight up to a large ledge that crosses the entire face, at the base of the central cliff.

Up to this point the route presents some minor technical difficulties that are easily overcome; what follows is much more sustained. Overcome the first part of the central cliff by going straight up over some surprisingly good, but vertical, rock, past a bolt placed in the rock. The second part of the central cliff has some loose, rotten rock. Make a horizontal traverse to the right to pass a large, detached block about 20 meters (65 ft) high. Move about 5 meters (15 ft) to the left once above the block to a good stance. Continue up the slope above to the base of the final cliff. Make a horizontal traverse to the right, along the base of the upper cliff, for two pitches (rope lengths). The upper cliff is broken in this area by a large crack. The first half of this crack is easy, while the upper half consists of more big, loose blocks that must be overcome. Continue to the summit of the Ventorrillo once the upper northeast ridge is reached.

It is also possible to continue traversing to the right along the base of the upper cliff to the shoulder that is west of the Ventorrillo.

The summit hut of Popocatépetl

Popocatépetl from Iztaccíhuatl

On the summit of Popo, with Ixta in background (Photo by Rich Weber)

The crater of Popocatépetl (Photo by Rich Weber)

Popocatépetl from Paso de Cortés (Photo by Ray Smutek)

Descending Las Cruces route, Tlamacas in right background (Photo by Rich Weber)

La Oeste de Popocatépetl (The West Face of Popocatépetl)

This route traverses across the lower west face before climbing its right-hand side to the summit. This is a long route. I estimate that it covers approximately 7 kilometers (4.2 mi) from Tlamacas; the El Ventorrillo route, by contrast, covers a little more than 4 kilometers (2.4 mi).

Leave the northeast ridge of the Ventorrillo at an approximate elevation of 4300 meters (14,100 ft) and traverse horizontally across the lower slopes of El Abanico del Ventorrillo. This is a long traverse, approximately 1.6 kilometers (1 mi) in length. At the far, western edge of the lower slope of El Abanico turn left and ascend to the lower west ridge of El Ventorrillo. Continue traversing south, across the lower west face of Popocatépetl, and gradually gain altitude, aiming for the right-hand (southern) edge of the west face. Climb the right side of the west face (40 degrees to 50 degrees in angle), and follow the crater rim left (north) to the summit. The most common error made when climbing this route is to start the traverse across El Abanico *too high*, which almost always results in unnecessary elevation loss. This route is only safe during the winter; some big avalanches and rock fall have occurred during other seasons.

The far southern edge of the west face has also been approached from the Teopixcalco hut, but this involves some elevation loss.

Climbing Routes on Iztaccíhuatl

Ixta is one of my three favorite high volcanoes. Although the standard route is long, it offers some route-finding difficulties and much more interest than the normal routes on Popo or Orizaba. Since the standard route is a traverse along many false summits and broad snowfields, as opposed to a straight climb up a volcanic cone, it is easy to get disoriented in a whiteout. Prudent climbers will take bearings and mark the route with wands to ensure a certain and safe return.

According to Aztec mythology, Iztaccíhuatl is known as "The Sleeping Lady," which can readily be understood when viewing the mountain from the west. The following terms for the parts of the mountain are in common use:

La Cabellera: the hair
La Cabeza: the head
La Oreja: the ear
El Cuello: the neck
El Pecho: the breast
La Barriga: the belly
Las Rodillas: the knees
Los Pies: the feet

At the Portillo, Iztaccíhuatl

Iztaccíhuatl from Paso de Cortés (Photo by Rich Weber)

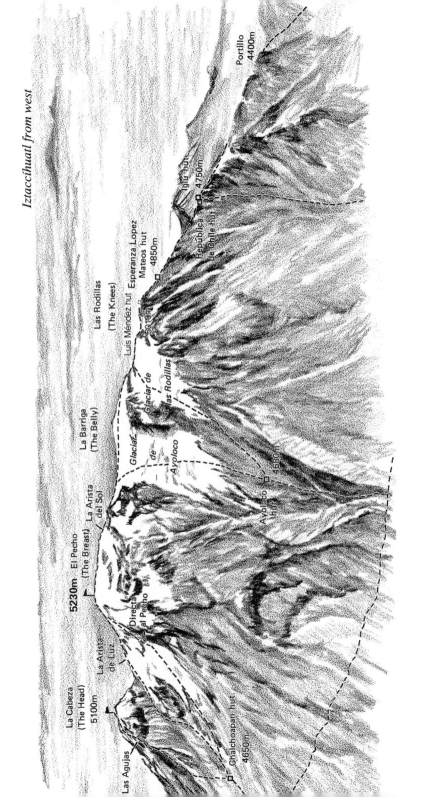

Iztaccihuatl from west

Portillo 4400m

Igu hut 4750m

República de Chile hut

Esperanza López Mateos hut 4850m

Luis Méndez hut 5010m

Las Rodillas (The Knees)

La Barriga (The Belly)

La Arista del Sol

Glaciar de las Rodillas

Glaciar de Ayoloco

Ayoloco hut 4680m

El Pecho (The Breast)

5230m

La Cabeza (The Head) 5100m

La Arista de Luz

Directa al Pecho

Chalchoapan hut 4650m

Las Agujas

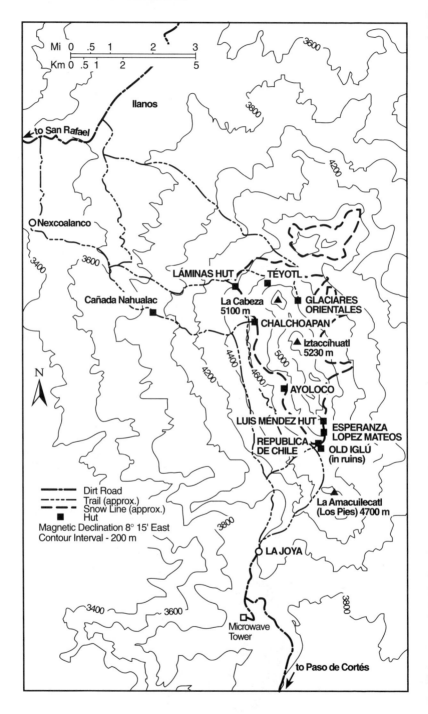

Mi 0 .5 1   2   3
Km 0 .5 1   2   5

llanos

to San Rafael

3600

3800

4200

O Nexcoalanco

3400   3600

Cañada Nahualac

LÁMINAS HUT   TÉYOTL

La Cabeza   GLACIARES
5100 m   ORIENTALES

CHALCHOAPAN

▲ Iztaccíhuatl
5230 m

4400   5000

4200   4600

AYOLOCO

N

LUIS MÉNDEZ HUT

ESPERANZA
LOPEZ MATEOS

REPUBLICA
DE CHILE   OLD IGLÚ
(in ruins)

▲ La Amacuilecatl
(Los Pies) 4700 m

Dirt Road
Trail (approx.)
Snow Line (approx.)
Hut
Magnetic Declination 8° 15' East
Contour Interval - 200 m

3800

O LA JOYA

3400   3600

3800

Microwave
Tower

to Paso de Cortés

The "head" and "breast" of Iztaccíhuatl from the west

La Cabeza
(The Head)
5100m

Las Agujas

La Oreja
Derecha

El Cuello
(The Neck)
5000m

La Arista
de Luz

Directa
al Pecho

4650m
Chalchoapan hut

5230m El Pecho
(The Breast)

La Arista
del Sol

Glaciar
de
Ayoloco

Ayoloco
hut

4680m

The Esperanza Lopez Mateos hut on Iztaccíhuatl; Popocatépetl in distance

Ixta is climbed from two major roadheads: La Joya (4000 m; 13,124 ft) from Paso de Cortés, and Nexcoalanco (3600 m; 11,811 ft) from the town of San Rafael, north of Amecameca.

La Joya is reached easily by means of a dirt road from Paso de Cortés. Many assume that the road ends at the microwave station, but it continues northward another 1.5 kilometers (0.9 mi) to the parking area, which is about a thirty-minute drive from Tlamacas. This roadhead leads to the huts in the vicinity of "the knees," as well as the Ayoloco and Chalchoapan huts on the western side of the mountain. La Joya has a bad reputation among climbers when the conversation turns to thieves. This approach is on the 1:50,000 Huejotzingo map, catalog number E14B42.

Nexcoalanco is harder to reach, but it offers the quickest approach to the routes on "the head." Highway 115 goes through Tlalmanalco before arriving in Amecameca. From the center of Tlalmanalco, drive approximately 6 kilometers (3.7 mi) east to the village of San Rafael. From here a steep, rough road climbs uphill to Nexcoalanco, where a climber's hut is located. Many climbers hire transportation in San Rafael or Amecameca to take them to Nexcoalanco. Others leave their vehicles in San Rafael and hike the 6 kilometers (3.7 mi) to the hut. San Rafael, as La Joya, also has a bad reputation when the conversation turns to thieves. This approach is shown on the 1:50,000 Amecameca and Huejotzingo maps, catalog numbers E14B41 and E14B42.

Another approach to the northern side of Ixta utilizes a road that begins at Pueblo Nuevo, a village halfway between Tlalmanalco and San Rafael. The road climbs north from Pueblo Nuevo, and passes above San Rafael. After passing through a forest with many switchbacks, the road ends in a "T" intersection (8.7 km; 5.4 mi from Pueblo Nuevo). Turn right, and go through some more switchbacks. About 3.5 kilometers (2.2 mi) after the intersection, a trail leaves the road to the right; 2 kilometers (1.2 mi) more take you to Nexcoalanco. Another kilometer farther on the main road, a large flat *llano* (plain) is reached and a trail leads toward the northern side of "the head" of Ixta. This approach is shown on the 1:50,000 Amecameca and Huejotzingo maps, catalog numbers E14B41 and E14B42.

Of the two roadheads, Nexcoalanco and La Joya, I prefer La Joya due to its simple approach and higher elevation. Most of the routes can be approached from the roadhead quite easily. Many years ago there was a small hut located here, but it has long since disappeared.

Rising above La Joya is a subsidiary peak of Iztaccíhuatl, La Amacuilecatl (also known as Los Pies or "the feet"). From the parking area, a trail leads straight uphill toward a cliff. After a short distance it angles left, gradually gaining elevation until the saddle between "the knees" and "the feet," the Portillo (Pass), is reached. Before arriving at the Portillo, the trail crosses a

Climbing to the Portillo, Iztaccíhuatl

small saddle at approximately 4400 meters (14,436 ft); a landmark for this saddle is a castlelike rock formation just to the left when facing the main summit of Ixta. (Many climbers bound for "the knees" huts have lost the trail and climbed over the top of this formation; minimum class 3.) Climb the ridge that rises above and left of this smaller saddle to the summit of "the feet." Another route on La Amacuilecatl starts at the Portillo, but soon leaves the ridge and traverses onto the northeast face. Both routes are class 3 to class 4. In the vicinity of La Joya, there are several other cliffs and crags that have class-5 routes. The rock is not especially bad, and it would be an interesting place to spend a free afternoon. All of the climbing routes on Iztaccíhuatl are on the 1:50,000 Huejotzingo map, catalog number E14B42.

La Arista del Sol (The Ridge of the Sun)
In the 1920s and 1930s a climber, Francisco Soto de Arroyo, pioneered some of the more difficult routes on the volcanoes, and gave unique names to their physical features. This name refers to the final ridge leading to the summit of Iztaccíhuatl. (Nevertheless, most climbers still refer to this route as "the knees" route.)

This is the standard route on the mountain, and since the nature of the climb is much different from climbs on the other volcanoes, this route is an enjoyable change. With Popo to one's back and El Pico de Orizaba to the east, the setting is exhilarating.

Between "the knees" and "the breast," four false summits are encountered. It is easy to get lost on these long, flat snowfields; keep an eye on the clouds, take bearings, and mark your route of ascent. Another complication is the difficulty of retreating in the event of bad weather or altitude illness. It is tempting to make a quick descent to the west, but several cliffs and icefalls hamper the escape; this should be attempted only by those familiar with the mountain. It is best to descend Ixta via the route of ascent.

Some people take two days to climb Ixta, spending a night in one of the huts in the vicinity of "the knees." However, the peak can be climbed quite easily in a day from La Joya, and this may be preferable if there is an absence of snow on the peak. There is no running water at the huts, and sometimes there is not enough snow to melt for water; in fact, I once climbed this route in my tennis shoes under such conditions.

There are two approaches to the huts beneath "the knees." One involves hiking the trail that leads to the Portillo from the parking area at La Joya (see description above for "the feet"). From the Portillo, the trail stays on the eastern slope of the ridge, gradually climbing back onto the ridge before the huts are reached. It is necessary to climb over a small peak, and then drop 35 meters (120 ft) to get to the two lower huts, the old Iglú ruins and República de Chile (4750 m; 15,585 ft). A third hut is higher, located just below the prominent rock bank of "the knees"; the Esperanza Lopez Mateos

On La Arista del Sol, Iztaccíhuatl

refuge is at 4850 meters (15,912 ft). It takes from four to six hours to hike to these huts from La Joya.

The other approach to "the knees" huts involves hiking up the western slope below the huts. From La Joya, a trail leads north and slightly downhill across a wide, grassy valley. The trail then climbs to a small saddle. From the saddle, turn right and start climbing uphill, passing a prominent cliff on its right side, to reach the two lower huts. Several other trails traverse across the western slope of the mountain. The most prominent trail across the western slope continues northward from the saddle north of La Joya, and leads to the Chalchoapan huts. Another trail traverses high on the western side of the mountain to the Ayoloco hut.

Above the huts, it is necessary to negotiate the cliff that marks "the knees." The preferred way involves climbing the snow on the left side of the cliff, but often there is not enough snow to cover the scree adequately. Should this be the case, it is better to climb the class-2 to class-3 rocks to the right. There is a hut on top of "the knees," the Luis Méndez hut (5010 m; 16,437 ft), which is shaped like an igloo. From the top of the Rodillas, climb over several false summits to the anti-climactic snowdome that marks the apex of the seventh highest peak of North America. The ascent takes from four to six hours from the huts. Ice axes and crampons should be carried, but may not be needed.

Glaciar de las Rodillas (The Knees Glacier)

This route starts at the Ayoloco hut (4690 m; 15,387 ft), beneath the Ayoloco Glacier on the western side of the mountain. This hut can be reached either by traversing and descending from the huts below "the knees," or by climbing up from one of the trails that traverses across the west side of the mountain. Above the Ayoloco hut there are two glaciers, separated by a rock cliff. To the right of these rocks is the Glaciar de las Rodillas, and the route climbs directly up this glacier, zigzagging through crevasses. Near the top, traverse to the left toward the Pecho, where a long walk leads to the summit. The angles can become very steep among the crevasses, and axes, crampons, ropes, and crevasse rescue equipment should be carried.

Glaciar de Ayoloco (Ayoloco Glacier)

This is believed to be the route of the first ascent of Ixta, first climbed by James de Salis in 1889. From the Ayoloco hut, climb straight up the glacier. Crevasses and small ice cliffs may bar the way, but can be passed easily. No false summits are encountered, and for climbers of moderate experience, this route is preferable to "the knees" route.

The Breast has been climbed via the rock cliff to the left of the Ayoloco Glacier, but there is a lot of rockfall off this cliff, and the climb is not recommended.

Directa al Pecho (Direct to the Breast)

This route climbs the northwest face of the main summit, "the breast." At first glance, it appears to be a straightforward, 700-meters (2,300 ft), 40-degrees, snow-and-ice climb, but several obstacles are not visible when

The "breast" and "head" of Iztaccihuatl from the east

5230m

La Arista
del Sol

La Cabeza.
(The Head)

5100m

El Cuello
(The Neck)
5000m

La Arista de Luz

La Arista
del Sol

1 2 3 4 5 6

To Teyotl hut

4800m

Glaciares
Orientales
hut

Routes on
Las Inescalables
de la Cabellera

1- La Oreja Izquierda
2- Hernando Manzanos
3- Otis McAllister
4- G.A.M.
5- Eduardo San Vicente
6- La Ruta del Sol

viewing the face from the Chalchoapan huts. Several small ice cliffs bar the way low on the face, and the angle steepens appreciably about 250 meters (800 ft) below the summit. Here a rock band bars the way, and the easiest route passes it on its left side; many intimidated parties traverse to The Ridge of Light to finish the climb.

Two variations of this climb have been done. One climbs through the rock band by traversing across it on a ledge from the left to the right before climbing the snow/ice slope above. The other more difficult and somewhat dangerous variation climbs the rocks on the far right-hand side of the face; there is a lot of loose rock on this latter variation.

La Arista de Luz (The Ridge of Light)

This route is also called El Cuello or "the neck" route, but Francisco Soto's imaginative name is used here.

From Nexcoalanco a trail leads around a ridge to Cañada Nahualac. The trail switchbacks at 3700 meters (12,150 ft), but another trail continues up the canyon, crosses a ridge, and continues uphill to the Chalchoapan huts, located at 4600 meters (15,100 ft) on the moraine of the glacier leading to "the neck." These huts can also be reached from La Joya by following the trail leading across the western slope of Ixta.

From the Chalchoapan huts, hike across the moraine to the glacier, then climb to the saddle ("the neck") between "the head" and the main summit; the angle averages 30 degrees. From "the neck," "the head" is a short distance away; a short class-3 section must be negotiated. The Arista de Luz leads to the main summit from "the neck" and offers little difficulty; but beware of crevasses that cross this ridge!

Las Agujas (The Needles)

Looking north from Chalchoapan, a ridge can be seen leading to "the head." On the lower portion of this ridge are several pinnacles that may be climbed for their own sake. Bypass the needles on their left sides and climb up the slopes on the left side of this ridge. This ridge dead ends against a small, rock wall; bypass it on its left side. Continue up and left to the final, short rock step (class 4) that is just below the summit of "the head." This route is much more pleasant when there is snow covering the abundant sand and gravel.

La Oreja Derecha (The Right Ear)

A more appropriate name for this route might be "The Right Temple and Forehead." This route climbs the northwest flank of "the head." For this and the following routes, the usual approach is from the plains north of the mountain. It is also possible to reach this side of the mountain from the Chalchoapan huts. A trail leads north from Chalchoapan across the lower,

Between Las Rodillas and La Barriga, Iztaccíhuatl

La Arista del Sol, Ixta

On La Arista del Sol, Iztaccíhuatl

The Luis Méndez hut on Iztaccíhuatl

gentle ridge of Las Agujas and then drops 200 meters (650 ft) to the Láminas hut (4440 m; 14,567 ft). Traverse eastward up and across the lower slopes of "the head" until almost due north of its summit. Turn right (south) through a field of talus, followed by sand and gravel, to reach the lower snow slopes of the route. Pass the two lower rock bands on their left sides, and cross the third rock band through a shallow chute; this chute is frequently filled with snow, and in this case it is easily overcome. Continue upward to the fourth big rock band. Upon reaching it, move slightly right to a break in the wall and climb a short (10 m; 33 ft) class-5 rock pitch, followed by a ramp of snow leading to the much larger ramp beneath the higher, fifth rock band. Follow this large ramp up and left to the summit.

As a variation, it is possible to avoid the rock bands completely by ascending the large ramp that leads up and left to the summit. This is the usual descent route from the summit of "the head" to the huts on the north side of Ixta.

Either of these approaches is much more aesthetically pleasing when there is a snow cover.

Las Inescalables de La Cabellera (The Unclimbable Routes of the Hair)

This does not refer to any specific route, but rather to the collection of routes on the northeastern side of "the head." A trail from the *llanos* north of Ixta leads to the saddle northeast of "the head." From the saddle, it is possible to reach the ruins of the Glaciares Orientales hut. By continuing up the ridge from the saddle, the Téyotl hut is reached. The northeast ridge itself leads to the 100-meters (330 ft), class-4 to class-5 rock routes on "the head." The ridge is mostly scree and tedious hiking. Underneath the northeast face, the ridge ends in a rock buttress. Traverse across the right side of the buttress and surmount it on its northern side. From here three routes present themselves. La Oreja Izquierda (The Left Ear) traverses across the face to the left and then climbs the east ridge of "the head." The Hernando Manzanos route (named after one of the climbers who died shortly after completing this route's first ascent) climbs the face immediately above the buttress; this was the first route climbed on the Cabellera (in the mid-1950s). The Otis McAllister route climbs farther to the right of the Manzanos route.

There are also three routes on the far right-hand face; it is better to traverse across the face to reach their bases, instead of climbing the afore-mentioned buttress. The G.A.M. route is named after the Grupo Alta Montaña (The High Mountain Group) of the Club de Exploraciones de México. Eduardo San Vicente participated in five foreign expeditions before meeting with tragedy on Mount Victoria in the Canadian Rockies in 1954, and a route is named after him. The third route is known as La Ruta del Sol (The Route of the Sun).

"The neck" can easily be reached from the east.

El Pico de Orizaba from the north; Piedra Grande in left foreground

CHAPTER FOUR

EL PICO DE ORIZABA

El Pico de Orizaba has a completely different character from Iztaccíhuatl or Popocatépetl. Popo and Ixta lie between two of the largest cities in Mexico, and one can look out from them to see sprawling urban areas. In contrast, El Pico de Orizaba is surrounded by Indian villages, many of which can only be reached by trail. It is necessary to pass through a few of these villages to approach the mountain, and anyone who spends a little time in them soon finds that Spanish is the inhabitants' second language with Indian languages their native tongue.

The strongest impression that one has while climbing this mountain is one of solitude and isolation. Untrained eyes have difficulty identifying signs of humanity's presence while looking at the plains below. Popocatépetl, Iztaccíhuatl, and La Malinche can be seen to the west, and the Gulf of

Mexico can be seen 60 miles to the east. I do not know of any other location in North America where the climate varies between tropical jungles and arctic snow in such a short distance. One has a powerful and fascinating feeling of height while standing on the summit.

The normal route on El Pico de Orizaba is on the north side of the mountain, over the Jamapa Glacier. The standard camp for this route is Piedra Grande, where two huts are located, along with (as far as I know) the only year-round source of running water on the mountain above timberline. During the latter part of the dry season, from January through April, the Jamapa Glacier is the only viable route to the summit because of this source of water. During the early climbing season, from late September to December, the other routes are much easier to climb, because snow patches can be easily located as sources of water. It is advantageous to hire a local guide when climbing the other routes to facilitate approaches and to locate water.

There are now two approaches to Piedra Grande, one from the east and one from the west. The western approach starts at the town of Tlachichuca. Head east from Puebla toward Veracruz on Highway 150-D, and get off the

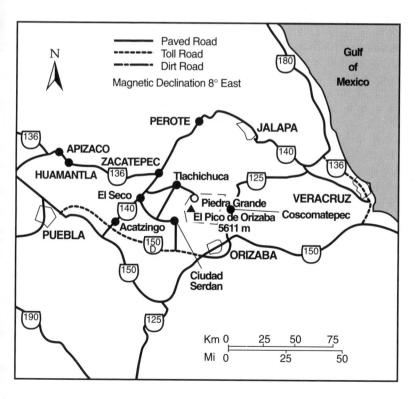

toll road approximately 40 kilometers (24.9 mi) from Puebla, where there is a sign showing the turnoff to Highway 140, which leads north to Jalapa. The turnoff ends in a traffic circle underneath the highway. Go left, drive underneath the toll road, taking care to avoid driving back onto the toll road by accident, and continue north another 2 kilometers (1.2 mi) to the town of Acatzingo, where the market is held on Tuesdays. Highway 140 originates in Puebla and offers a scenic (and free) alternative to the toll road.

Take the highway bypass around Acatzingo and drive another 27 kilometers (16.8 mi) north on Highway 140 to the town of El Seco. Continue another 7 kilometers (4.3 mi) to a signed intersection pointing the way to Tlachichuca. Turn right; Tlachichuca is another 22 kilometers (13.7 mi).

Tlachichuca (2600 m; 8,530 ft) is the end of the paved road, and its citizens have been serving the needs of climbers from all over the globe for many years now. Supplies can be purchased here, modest lodging is available, and the restaurant most popular with tourists is the Casa Blanca, located at the north corner of the plaza, between the marketplace and the city hall.

Previous editions of this book have given detailed driving instructions to Piedra Grande, the base camp for the Jamapa Glacier route. These directions are not included in this edition, mainly because the route changes every year. It is a very rough and bumpy dirt road. When it is dry, it is so dusty that it is difficult to see past the windshield, and when it is wet, the volcanic soil is very slick and it is difficult to get traction. I now tell people that the road has become "class 6 with a two-wheel-drive vehicle"; in other words, one almost always has to get out and push the car up an especially nasty section. Most disturbing of all has been the number of rental cars, driven by climbers, that have been wrecked attempting to drive to Piedra Grande. Mexican rental-car insurance does not cover vehicles driven on dirt roads, and I can only assume that these financial losses must have put a real dent in these individuals' peak-bagging plans for a long time.

Four-wheel-drive taxi service has been available in Tlachichuca for many years, and the Reyes family has been providing this service for climbers for the longest time. In addition, the Reyes family has constructed a very comfortable and secure dormitory for climbers in Tlachichuca; hot showers are available here, but there is a water shortage in the village, so please don't abuse this privilege. The Reyes family can also give you the most up-to-date bus schedules, and can help you locate guides, pack animals, and supplies that climbers need. Their services are in great demand, and two- to three-month advance reservations are suggested. The Reyes can be reached by writing them via Mexico City c/o Francisco Reyes R., Santiago 344, San Jerónimo Lídice, 10200 México D.F., México. From telephones in the United States, the Mexico City telephone numbers are the international access code + 52-5-595-1203 or 52-5-595-3206; the fax number is the international access code + 52-5-681-7306.

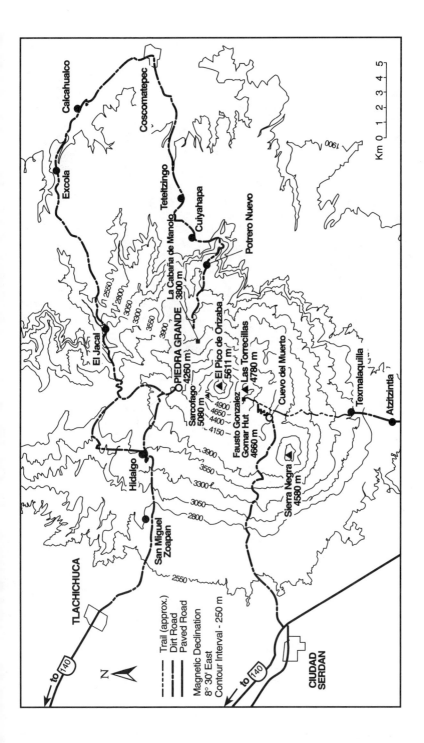

El Pico de Orizaba from Piedra Grande

Those without advance reservations can contact the Reyes family directly through the store, formerly named La Antigua Flor, at Calzada Jesús Ortega Sur No. 1, 75050 Tlachichuca, Puebla, México. This store is now unnamed, but it is located across the street from the PEMEX station at the corner of Calzada Jesús Ortega and Avenida Francisco Madero in Tlachichuca.

Four-wheel-drive taxi service is also available in Tlachichuca from Señor Joaquin Canchola L., Calle 3 Poniente No. 3, 75050 Tlachichuca, Puebla, México.

Those not wishing to take advantage of these taxi services can hike the 23 kilometers (14 mi) with 1620 meters (5,300 ft) of elevation gain to Piedra Grande. This is a pleasant hike, passing through fields of corn and potatoes and the village of Hidalgo, which I believe is the highest community in North America at 3400 meters (11,155 ft) above sea level. Another option is to take the four-wheel-drive taxi one way only, and hike back down to Tlachichuca, or continue the hike in the opposite direction, down to the city of Coscomatepec, which serves as the base for the eastern approach to Piedra Grande. This approach is shown on the 1:50,000 San Salvador El Seco and Coscomatepec sheets, catalog numbers E14B45 and E14B46.

Perhaps the easiest approach to Coscomatepec is from the city of Veracruz, taking Highway 150 past the city of Córdoba to the smaller city of Fortín de las Flores. Drive north from Fortín on Highway 125 for 17 kilometers (10.2 mi) to Coscomatepec.

Those approaching Coscomatepec from Mexico City and Puebla travel east on the toll road Highway 150-D. You will leave the Mexican plateau soon after passing the Esperanza toll booth, and the road curves and switchbacks a long way down to the major industrial city of Orizaba before arriving at the junction with Highway 125, just north of Fortín de las Flores. In less than an hour, one drops from a temperate to a tropical climate. Drive north on Highway 125 for 17 kilometers (10.2 mi) to the city of Coscomatepec.

Coscomatepec (1540 m; 5,050 ft) is a pleasant, small city with a beautiful plaza, and snowcapped El Pico de Orizaba viewed to the west between palm trees is very impressive. Market day is Monday, and the El Rey restaurant at the corner of Boulevard Bravo and Highway 125 is very popular with tourists. The Hotel San Antonio is located across from the main plaza of Coscomatepec at Nicolas Bravo 35 (from telephones in the United States, dial the international access code + 52-273-70-320). Contact Señor Manuel Gutierrez A., Calle Juárez 8, 94140 Coscomatepec, Veracruz, México for information on four-wheel-drive transportation to Piedra Grande or Ojo Salado. From telephones in the United States, his phone numbers are the international access code + 52-273-70-020, 52-273-70-126, or 52-273-70-193.

Drive north from Coscomatepec on the road that leads past the cemetery (you don't have to major in English to understand symbolism) and drive

The plaza at Coscomatepec

Loading the truck in Coscomatepec

The Octavio Alvarez hut at Piedra Grande

The Augusto Pellet hut at Piedra Grande, El Pico de Orizaba

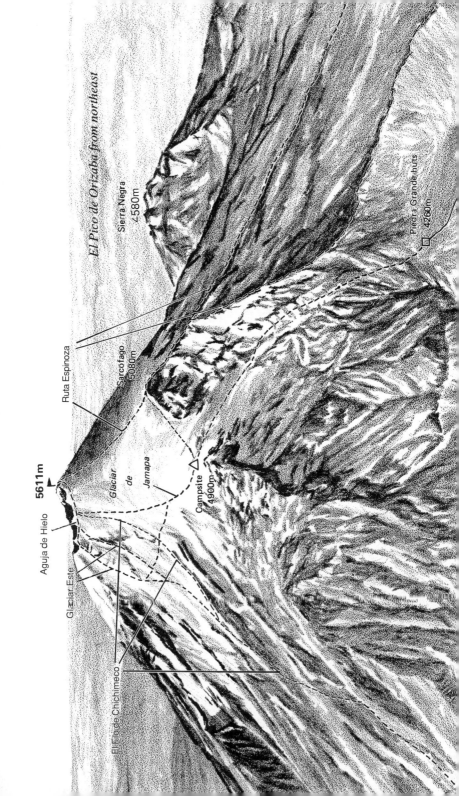

El Pico de Orizaba from northeast

5611m

Aguja de Hielo

Glaciar Este

El Filo de Chichimeco

Glaciar de Jamapa

Ruta Espinoza

Sarcofago 5080m

Sierra Negra ∠580m

Campsite 4900m

Piedra Grande huts 4260m

El Pico de Orizaba from east

▲ 5611m

Ruta Espinoza

Aguja de Hielo

Glaciar de Jamapa

△ Campsite 4900m

Glaciar Este

El Filo de Chichimeco

through the villages of Tozongo and Acolco. A bridge crosses the remarkably deep canyon of the Río Cuapa and then climbs to the lovely village of Calcahualco, which features a divided main street with hedges carved into animal figures. The road continues up the crest of the ridge that divides the

El Sarcófago, El Pico de Orizaba (Photo by Rich Weber)

Market day in Coscomatepec

Río Jamapa from the Río Cuapa, and a major fork is encountered just beyond the village of Excola. The fork to the right leads down to the village of Atotonilco, deep in the canyon of the Jamapa River, where there are some hot springs.

Take the left fork and continue up the road along the ridgecrest, passing through the villages of Totzinapa and Tecuanapa to another fork. The left fork leads to the village of Vaquería. Take the right fork through the village of Tlacotiopa (2800 m; 9,186 ft). This is the limit for most two-wheel-drive vehicles. Drive through Tlacotiopa to the village of El Jacal at 3000 meters (9,840 ft) above sea level, where the road leaves the ridge and moves to its left side. The road then fords the Jamapa River (just a minor stream at this point), and climbs with many switchbacks before crossing a major ridge. Beyond the ridge the road forks; the right fork leads down to the village of Hidalgo (the last village of the western approach to Piedra Grande from Tlachichuca). Take the left fork to Piedra Grande. The road crosses another ridge and later meets the main road coming up from Hidalgo and Tlachichuca. Go left to the Piedra Grande huts. This approach is on the 1:50,000 Coscomatepec sheet, catalog number E14B46.

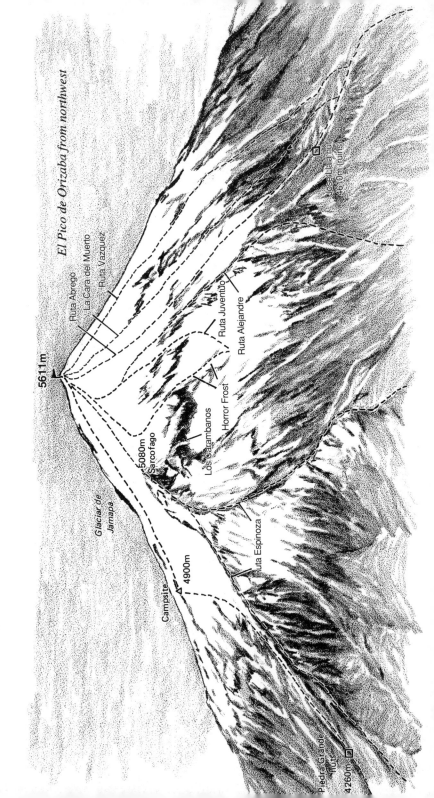

El Pico de Orizaba from northwest

5611m

Ruta Abrego
La Cara del Muerto
Ruta Vazquez

Ruta Juventino
Ruta Alejandre

Horror Frost

Los Carambanos

5080m
Sarcofago

Glaciar de
Jamapa

Ruta Espinoza

Campsite
4900m

José Lilla hut
4610m (ruins)

Piedra Grande
Huts
4260m

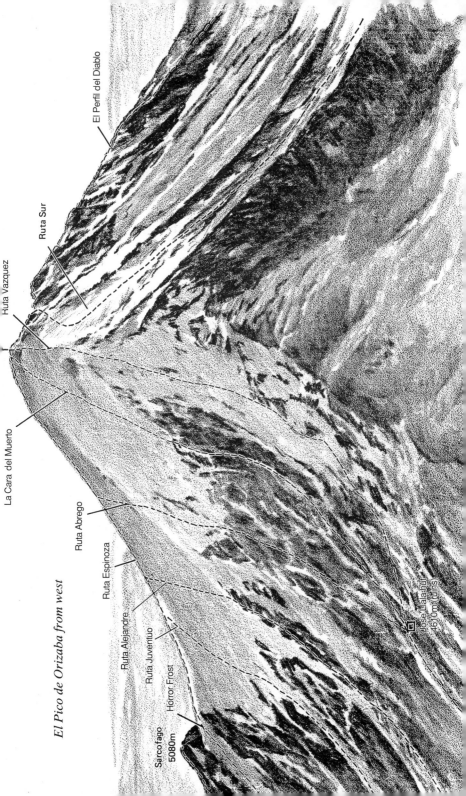

El Pico de Orizaba from west

El Perfil del Diablo

Ruta Sur

Ruta Vazquez

La Cara del Muerto

Ruta Abrego

Ruta Espinoza

Ruta Alejandre

Ruta Juventuo

Horror Frost

Sarcofago
5080m

Jose Tlalahui
4610m (ruins)

Which is the best approach to Piedra Grande? The shortest, most direct route is on the west side of the mountain, from Tlachichuca. There are also more services for climbers available in Tlachichuca, and its elevation (2600 m; 8,530 ft) makes it better suited for acclimatization. But the more scenic and interesting approach is from Coscomatepec, on the eastern slope of the mountain. This 36-kilometer (22-mi) approach starts in the tropics, ends above timberline, and climbs among awesome canyons with tremendous vertical relief.

Climbing Routes on El Pico de Orizaba

Glaciar de Jamapa (Jamapa Glacier)
This is the standard, normal route on the mountain. Other names used are Ruta Norte or Northern Route and Cara Norte or North Face. There is a flat parking area just below the level of Piedra Grande (4260 m; 13,976 ft); unload four-wheel-drive trucks here and walk uphill to the two huts.

La Aguja de Hielo on El Pico de Orizaba

Approaching the summit of Orizaba, Glaciar de Jamapa (Photo by Rich Weber)

The older structure, the Augusto Pellet hut, is made out of corrugated metal, and as many as twelve have fit into its various sleeping shelves. The newer hut, Octavio Alvarez, is a large stone structure with room for over sixty people. The park service, El Grupo de Los Cien, and the local jeep drivers maintain both of these huts, and they should be in good repair long into the future. There is also a tent platform nearby, to accommodate everyone on really crowded weekends, and an outhouse.

There is no running water in the immediate vicinity of Piedra Grande. The water source is nearby, however, off to the left (east) of the Augusto Pellet hut. A trail leads down to a small tank with a hose that flows continuously. I like to think that this is the source of the 112-kilometer (67 mi) Jamapa River, which empties into the Gulf of Mexico south of Veracruz.

There is a large iron cross near the Augusto Pellet hut, and this marks the start of the trail to the Jamapa Glacier. The well-worn trail leads to the right of a prominent gully. Follow the trail upward to meet the first stone aqueduct at 4360 meters (14,300 ft). Go left along the top of this aqueduct for 25 meters (80 ft) to its end, and climb the slope directly above. You should meet the second aqueduct at a distinctive break in its wall at 4450 meters (14,600 ft). Go left along the top of the second aqueduct for 50 meters (165 ft) to its end, marked by a covered stone tank with plastic outlet pipes at 4460 meters (14,640 ft). A series of dark cliffs can be seen from here when facing the

Interior of the Octavio Alvarez hut, El Pico de Orizaba

summit of the mountain. Bypass these by climbing up and to the right (a 100-degree turn to the right from the direction that the aqueduct flows from). This leads to a small moraine in a bare, rocky valley. Continue up the valley to a flat area at approximately 4900 meters (16,000 ft); some parties camp here to shorten the ascent.

The glacier starts here, and it would be best to rope up, as many climbers have found several hidden crevasses. Continue climbing the glacier, which at times is steep, and aim for the right-hand rocks on the crater rim. (The rock pinnacle to the left is the Aguja de Hielo or Ice Needle, a prominent landmark). Traverse across these rocks to the right for approximately 200 meters (656 ft), then go up to the crater rim. Hike around the rim to the high point, marked by a cross. The ascent should take from four to seven hours from Piedra Grande. This route is on the 1:50,000 Coscomatepec map, catalog number E14B46.

Ruta Espinoza (Espinoza Route)

This route could be considered a variation of the Jamapa Glacier route. It follows the rounded ridge that rises above the col south of the Sarcófago, a rocky, volcanic peak to the north of the true summit of El Pico de Orizaba. Follow the Jamapa Glacier route from Piedra Grande and climb onto the lower portion of the glacier. As soon as practical, turn right and head for the saddle south of the Sarcófago. Turn left upon arriving at the saddle, and follow the rounded ridge directly to the crater rim. This route is on the 1:50,000 Coscomatepec map, catalog number E14BH46.

Two significant variations of this route have been done. Both involve traversing over the top of the Sarcófago. Two ridges lead to the Sarcófago, one from the north and one from the west. The northern ridge is best approached by leaving the Piedra Grande road at an approximate elevation of 4400 meters (14,435 ft). The western ridge is approached from the village of Hidalgo; go south from the village for about 1½ kilometers (1 mi) to the Barranca Alpinahua, and climb this canyon to its head, which leads to the crest of the western ridge of the Sarcófago. Both of these variations are much more pleasant with snow cover. The San Salvador El Seco 1:50,000 map is needed for the approach to the western ridge, in addition to the Coscomatepec sheet, catalog numbers E14B45 and E14B46.

Los Carámbanos (The Icicles)

On occasion, some vertical, frozen waterfalls form on the west face of the Sarcófago. One of these waterfalls was climbed by Barry Blanchard and Mark Barrow on January 10, 1988. A high camp is necessary when climbing these from Hidalgo. The approach and route are on the San Salvador El Seco and Coscomatepec maps, catalog numbers E14B45 and E14B46.

Horror Frost

This route climbs the northwest-facing amphitheater between the Sarcófago and the main peak of El Pico de Orizaba. It was first climbed in a bold solo effort by Jared Israels on December 29, 1978.

Go south from the village of Hidalgo for about 2½ kilometers (1½ mi), across the Barranca Alpinahua to the next major canyon; this latter canyon is south of the west ridge of the Sarcófago. Go up the canyon to a high camp at 4400 meters (14,400 ft). While looking at the amphitheater, one can see two ramps that slope up to the left. The Horror Frost route follows the left-hand ramp. From the top of this ramp, a 100-foot couloir at an angle of 60 degrees leads to the col south of the Sarcófago. This route was named following its first ascent for the hoar-frost conditions found in this exit couloir. The approach and route are on the San Salvador El Seco and Coscomatepec maps, catalog numbers E14B45 and E14B46.

Ruta Juventud (Youth Route)

This route also climbs the northwest amphitheater of El Pico de Orizaba, only it follows the right-hand ramp mentioned above. It was first climbed in

April 1962 by a team from the Socorro Alpino de México, which included Gabriel Caballero, Alfonso Alvarez, Carlos Castillo, Ruben García, David Aguero, and Jorge Rodea. Slide up sand and scree slopes from a high camp to the base of the cliff that marks the right-hand ramp, and follow the ramp through the cliffs before meeting the Espinoza Route. Climb this latter route to the summit. This route and its approach are on the San Salvador El Seco and Coscomatepec maps, catalog numbers E14B45 and E14B46.

Ruta Alejandre

This route is on the left-hand side of the west face of El Pico de Orizaba. The approach begins by going south from the village of Hidalgo, past the first major canyon, Barranca Alpinahua, to the next major canyon, as described above under the Horror Frost and Juventud routes. Climb onto the wide ridge on the left side of this canyon, gaining its broad crest at a relatively low elevation (approximately 3500 m; 11,483 ft), and follow it uphill. Gradually move right in the basin above this canyon, and climb onto the shallow ridge that marks the right side of this basin; a camp is usually placed somewhere along this ridge.

At approximately 5000 meters (16,400 ft) leave the ridge by making a diagonal traverse up and left across the west face of El Pico de Orizaba. Once one is well beyond, and slightly above, the shallow gully low on this face, turn right, and make a direct ascent of the shallow snow rib to the top. One should come to the crater rim right at the high point of the mountain, marked by the iron cross. This route and its approach are on the San Salvador El Seco and Coscomatepec maps, catalog numbers E14B45 and E14B46.

Ruta Abrego

This route ascends the central portion of the west face of El Pico de Orizaba. One approaches this route, and the following two routes, by hiking about 5 kilometers (3 mi) south from Hidalgo to the maze of canyons in the vicinity of Barranca El Carnero. This is shown on the San Salvador El Seco and Coscomatepec maps, catalog numbers E14B45 and E14B46. Climb onto the major ridge rising above these canyons, and follow it upward to the ruins of the José Llaca hut at 4610 meters (15,125 ft); a camp is usually placed here. Continue up the ridge to where it abuts the lobe of the Glaciar Occidente at approximately 5000 meters (16,400 ft). Climb the glacier to the crater rim, and follow the rim to the high point.

La Cara del Muerto (The Face of Death)

This route has also been called Club de Exploraciones de México. It climbs the loose rock face to the right of the Ruta Abrego. Leave the major ridge arising from the Barranca El Carnero at an altitude of 4600 meters (15,100 ft). Climb the loose scree and sand slope to the right of the ridge,

On the summit of El Pico de Orizaba

making a slight traverse to the right. At about 5000 meters (16,400 ft) go left and directly ascend the slope above to the summit.

Ruta Vázquez

This route climbs the southwest glacier on El Pico de Orizaba before joining the southern route. Leave the major ridge rising above the Barranca El Carnero at 4600 meters (15,100 ft) and make a diagonal ascending traverse to the right, aiming for the glacier on the southwest side of the peak. Climb the glacier, but keep to the west side of the ridge to the right, until reaching the crater rim. Follow the rim north to the summit.

Ruta Sur (Southern Route)

This is the old standard route on Orizaba, used before construction of the road to Piedra Grande in the early 1960s. There are now two approaches for this route: one via a four-wheel-drive track from Ciudad Serdán, and the other via trail from the village of Texmalaquilla.

Ciudad Serdán can be reached by a number of routes. A highway leaves Highway 140 at the town of El Seco, and heads southeast for 29 kilometers (17.4 mi) to Ciudad Serdán. There is also a paved road that leads southwest out of Tlachichuca to meet this highway north of Ciudad Serdán. A third option is to leave Highway 150-D at the Esperanza toll booth and head north for 18 kilometers (10.8 mi) toward Ciudad Serdán; the roads around this toll booth are confusing, so one must take care not to head south toward the city of Tehuacan by accident! Four-wheel-drive service can be obtained in Ciudad Serdán by contacting Señor Enrique Ramírez Juárez, 3 Poniente 517, 75520 Ciudad Serdán, Puebla, México; from telephones in the United States, he can be reached by dialing the international access code + 52-245-20-579. A small hotel east of Señor Juárez's home is the Posada Maria Isabel, and a popular restaurant with tourists is La Unión, located across the street from the main church in Ciudad Serdán.

From Ciudad Serdán (2550 m; 8,366 ft), the four-wheel-drive route starts by following a paved road east to where it ends in the village of San Francisco Cuautlancingo. Continue up a dirt road to the village of San Martín Ojo de Agua, the limit for most two-wheel-drive cars. The four-wheel-drive track goes east, climbing the long canyon leading to the saddle (4020 m; 13,189 ft) between Sierra Negra and El Pico de Orizaba. The road continues east about 100 meters (300 ft) beyond the three crosses that mark the saddle to a fork. Take the left fork. The road then switchbacks up this ravine to an approximate elevation of 4500 meters (14,750 ft), where it ends. Then follow a trail for 1 kilometer (0.6 mi) and 150 meters (500 ft) of gain to the Fausto Gonzalez Gomar hut at 4660 meters (15,288 ft).

The other approach to the Fausto Gonzalez Gomar hut begins from the village of Texmalaquilla (3100 m; 10,170 ft), which is reached via a dirt road from the village of Atzitzintla. Atzitzintla can be reached via a paved road from the highway that leads south of Ciudad Serdán. A steep trail leads north from Texmalaquilla for 10 kilometers with 1500 meters of gain (6 mi; 4,920 ft) to the hut.

By either approach, the stone Fausto Gonzalez Gomar hut has room for about forty people on wooden bunk beds. There is no permanent, continuous source of water at the hut, and the best time of year to climb this route is at the end, and immediately after, the summer rainy season, from late September to early December. During this period there is the possibility that patches of snow can be located near the hut to provide water for dehydrated climbers.

Follow a good use trail (the one that climbers have defined by using it so much) from the hut to approximately 4880 meters (16,000 ft). Climb up and left into the gully that descends from the summit; this gully is bounded by two small rock buttresses. This is a much better climb when the gully is filled with snow. Ascend the gully (or the rock buttresses) to a rock outcrop beneath the crater rim. Skirt the rock band on the left; the actual summit is 10 meters (33 ft) higher and 100 meters (328 ft) beyond the point where the crater rim is first reached. The summit is five to seven hours from the Fausto Gonzalez Gomar hut.

The classic camp for the Southern Route has been Cueva del Muerto. When approaching the pass between Sierra Negra and El Pico de Orizaba from Ciudad Serdán, a broad, rocky ridge can be seen to the left. The cave is on the far side of the ridge, about 1½ kilometers (1 mi) east of the pass. It is situated among trees beneath overhanging rocks on a long shelf about 10 meters (33 ft) wide, on the left side of a wide grassy valley. All approaches to this route are covered by the Orizaba, Ciudad Serdán, San Salvador El Seco, and Coscomatepec maps, catalog numbers E14B56, E14B55, E14B45, and E14B46.

One cannot help but notice two prominent peaks to the south of El Pico de Orizaba, Las Torrecillas and Sierra Negra. Las Torrecillas, at 4780 meters (15,682 ft), is a fine scramble; these little towers are just southeast of the Fausto Gonzalez Gomar hut. Sierra Negra (4580 m; 15,026 ft) is a class-2 ascent from the saddle between it and El Pico de Orizaba.

El Perfil del Diablo (The Devil's Profile)

This is the next ridge to the east from the Southern Route. Climb to the saddle north of Las Torrecillas from the Fausto Gonzalez Gomar hut. Traverse east from the saddle to the prominent ridge to the east. Follow the ridge north to the crater rim, and follow the crater rim around to the left to the summit. All approaches to this route are covered by the Orizaba, Ciudad Serdán, San Salvador El Seco, and Coscomatepec maps, catalog numbers E14B56, E14B55, E14B45, and E14B46.

Glaciar Este (Eastern Glacier)

This is, technically speaking, the most difficult route on the mountain. It is also known as Glaciares Orientales and El Pecho de la Paloma (Dove's Breast). It has been made famous by two articles that appeared in *Summit* magazine, an American publication.[10] This side of the mountain has two couloirs. The southern, or left-hand, couloir is wide, and it has an angle of 40 degrees. The right-hand couloir is narrow, exposed to rockfall, and about

---

10. Dan McCool, "Orizaba—The Other Side of the Mountain," *Summit*, Vol. 25, No. 3 (June-July 1979), pp. 9–11, and Rachel Cox, "Orizaba Alternatives," *Summit*, Vol. 33, No. 5 (Sept-Oct 1987), pp. 28–31. (The photograph on page 30 is printed backward.)

50 degrees steep. The easiest, and most popular, approach to these couloirs is from Piedra Grande. Climb the Jamapa Glacier to approximately 5000 meters (16,400 ft), and then traverse left (south) over the Filo de Chichimeco to the basin beneath the couloirs. Another approach uses the lower part of the Filo de Chichimeco from the Barranca Ojo Salado. From the top of either couloir, traverse to the right over the pinnacles along the crater rim to the summit. This route and its approach are covered by the Coscomatepec map, catalog number E14B46.

El Filo de Chichimeco (Chichimeco Ridge)

This route ascends the ridge between the Jamapa Glacier and the Eastern Glacier. The ridge can be approached from Piedra Grande over the Jamapa Glacier, but the classic approach starts from Coscomatepec, starting in the tropics, ending above timberline, and passing through several Indian villages and among awesome canyons with tremendous vertical relief. Drive west out of Coscomatepec on Calle Juárez.

The road leads through the villages of Ixtayuca, Boquerón, Tecóac, Teteltzingo, Cuiyachapa, to the small village of Potrero Nuevo (3250 m; 10,660 ft), the limit for most two-wheel-drive vehicles. The four-wheel-drive track actually leaves the main road just below Potrero Nuevo; it goes right, and after a steep climb it enters the lovely meadows of Ojo Salado. The road continues through the meadows to a fork. The right fork leads over the pass southwest of Cerro Chichimeco before dropping down to the villages of Vaquería and El Jacal on the northeast slope of the mountain. Take the left fork through the meadows and forest to where the road makes an abrupt descent to a streambed.

Leave the road here and hike up the ridge that is south (left) of the stream for about 1 kilometer (0.6 mi) to the mouth of the Barranca Ojo Salado. La Cabaña de Manolo (Manuel's Cabin) at 3800 meters (12,467 ft) is located here. Go to the right, away from the stream below the cabin, and hike up the steep slope behind the cabin. This slope eventually leads to El Filo de Las Dunas (The Ridge of the Dunes). This is actually a broad ridge, perhaps 200 meters (650 ft) wide, marked by a small, sharp ridge on its right and an obtuse edge on its left; the ridge lies to the right (north) of Barranca Ojo Salado. The name becomes obvious once one has risen above timberline and is hiking over disagreeably loose sand patches interspersed with tufts of grass.

The ridge at first climbs to the northwest before turning west and south-west toward the Filo de Chichimeco, which it meets at 4300 meters (14,100 ft); this is the best place to set up a high camp. At first, the Chichimeco ridge is covered with some big, loose blocks, followed by a narrow ridgecrest that leads upward toward the eastern edge of the Jamapa Glacier. Climb the left

Climbing El Filo de Chichimeco, El Pico de Orizaba

side of the glacier to the crater rim, meeting it between the Aguja de Hielo (Ice Needle) and the rocks leading to the main summit along the Jamapa Glacier route. This route and its approach are on the Coscomatepec map, catalog number E14B46.

La Malinche from Campamento IMSS La Malintzin

CHAPTER FIVE

LA MALINCHE AND NEVADO DE TOLUCA

These two peaks are east and west of Mexico City, and they are frequently used as training/acclimatization climbs by foreign mountaineers visiting Mexico whose main goal is to climb one or more of the three high volcanoes. They are worthwhile objectives for their own sake, and the natural beauty of their grass- and tree-covered slopes makes these mountains major objectives for self-propelled outdoor enthusiasts of all nationalities.

La Malinche (4462 m; 14,640 ft)

Before Cortés landed near Veracruz, his soldiers defeated a Mayan war party. The spoils of the victory included twenty young females. Among them was a beautiful and intelligent woman, whom the Indians called Malintzin, a title of honor meaning rain. The Spaniards mispronounced her name as Malinche, and she became Cortés wife, aide, and interpreter. Legends surround Malinche, the most popular being *La Llorona* (Weeping Woman). With long white robes and floor-length hair, her ghost is seen at night, crying in agony over the actions that resulted in the betrayal of her race 400 years ago.

La Malinche is east of Mexico City and north of Puebla. It has become my favorite acclimatization climb in recent years. It is high, access is very easy (either by private automobile or public transportation), and the hike to the summit covers just enough distance and elevation gain to provide a good workout and an opportunity to assess one's level of conditioning and acclimatization. Perhaps its main attraction is the Campamento IMSS La Malintzin, a government-operated resort located on the northern slope of the mountain. "Government-operated resort" may seem to be an oxymoron, like "jumbo

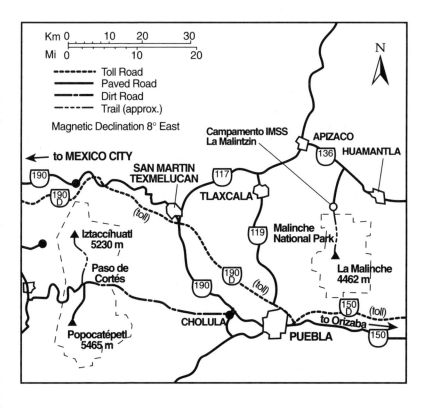

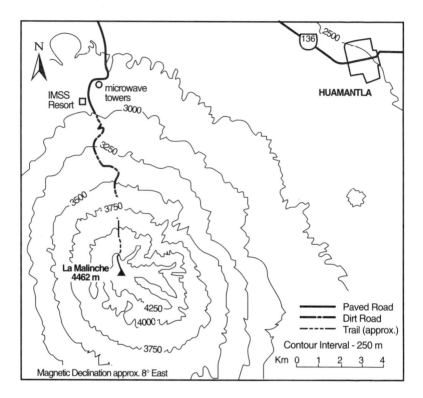

shrimp" or "military intelligence." But this resort is a nice place, with a campground, rental cabins with hot showers, a store, a restaurant serving excellent food, a playground, two soccer fields, and even a heliport. The cost is extremely reasonable, even on weekends, when the prices double and the place is packed to capacity.

From Puebla, drive north on Highway 119, past the city of Tlaxcala (famous for its woolen goods) to Apizaco. From Apizaco, take Highway 136 east approximately 13 kilometers (8 mi) to a signed junction, pointing the way to the IMSS resort; there is a *deadly* double curve just before this junction when driving from Apizaco. For those driving west on Highway 136, the junction is 13 kilometers (8 mi) from the city of Huamantla. From either Apizaco or Huamantla, turn off the highway at the junction and drive southwest. One enters a small village 4.3 kilometers (2.7 mi) after leaving Highway 136; turn left at a sign pointing the way to the microwave (*microondas*) station. Stay on the main road another 9 kilometers (5.6 mi) to the IMSS resort. The pavement ends just beyond the resort, and it is another 4.7 kilometers (2.9 mi) of rough dirt road to the roadhead.

The trail goes almost due south from the roadhead, making a direct ascent

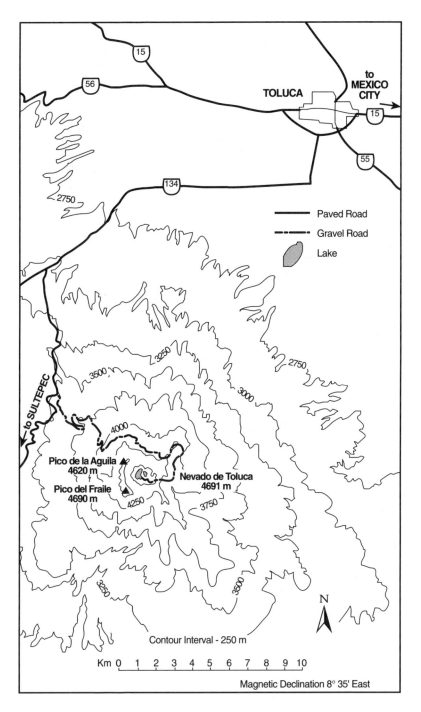

Looking down on Laguna del Sol from Pico del Fraile

of the slope above, passing some buildings in ruins. The trail is marked with "IMSS" signs as it climbs through the trees to the grassy basin north of the peak. The summit is reached after climbing to the ridge that connects the true summit of Malinche with its northern subsidiary rock peak. It is an easy scramble to the summit from the top of the ridge. The 4 kilometers (2.4 mi) and 1000 meters (3,300 ft) of elevation gain should take about three hours from the roadhead. The Tlaxcala and Puebla 1:50,000 maps, catalog numbers E14B33 and E14B43, are needed to do this hike.

Nevado de Toluca (4691 m; 15,390 ft)

This is Mexico's fourth highest mountain, and it is unique in that one can drive into the crater of this extinct volcano. The Aztec name for this mountain is Xinantecatl (The Naked Man). Nevado de Toluca has two summits, the higher named Pico del Fraile (Friar's Peak) at 4691 meters (15,390 ft) to the south, and Pico de la Aguila (Eagle's Peak) at 4620 meters (15,157 ft) on the northern side of the crater rim.

Take Highway 15 west from Mexico City toward the city of Toluca. Before reaching Toluca, take a bypass—Paseo Tollocan—leading south around the city. At the southern edge of Toluca, turn left (south) onto Highway 134, the main road leading into Toluca from the south. After 2 kilometers (1.2 mi), Highway 134 turns right, leading to Temascaltepec. Eighteen kilometers (11.2 mi) farther, Highway 3 branches off to the left toward Sultepec. Follow this road for 8 kilometers (5 mi) to a gravel road leading up the peak. Turn left off the highway and drive past a campground and dormitory-style lodge (both open to the public); after several switchbacks the road circles around the north side of the mountain to the east and eventually to the two lakes in the crater. These two lakes—the larger Laguna del Sol (Lake of the Sun) and the smaller Laguna de la Luna (Lake of the Moon)—are at 4200 meters (13,780 ft) above sea level. Perhaps what is most interesting about these lakes is that scuba diving is practiced in their 10-degrees C (50 degrees F) waters. Laguna del Sol offers trout fishing.

Pico del Fraile is 500 meters (1,600 ft) above the end of the road. The preferred routes of ascent are along the rim of the crater; the rock is much more sound on the ridges than on the faces beneath them. If there is a great deal of snow and ice, axes, crampons, and perhaps a rope should be carried. This mountain is on the 1:50,000 Volcán Nevado de Toluca map, catalog number E14A47.

APPENDIX A
RECOMMENDED READING

Backcountry Mexico: A Traveler's Guide and Phrase Book (1986) by Bob Burleson and David H. Riskind, University of Texas Press, Box 7819, Austin, Texas 78713. Highly recommended. This book has been written mainly for those interested in trekking in the northern part of Mexico. But the information it contains is applicable to all of Mexico's backcountry.

Backpacking in Mexico and Central America: A Guide for Walkers and Naturalists (1982), by Hilary Bradt and Rob Rachowiecki, Bradt Enterprises, 95 Harvey Street, Cambridge, Massachusetts 02140. In spite of the limited coverage given to Mexico, this book provides interesting, informative reading for those planning to visit the northern part of Latin America.

The People's Guide to Mexico (1990), by Carl Franz, John Muir Publications, P.O. Box 613, Santa Fe, New Mexico 87501. This is the definitive book that describes Mexico. All types of travelers will find it useful. Franz's *The People's Guide to Camping in Mexico* (1981) is now, unfortunately, out-of-print. This is not so much a guidebook on where to go but a guidebook on how to travel. Truly a great book, very readable, entertaining, and full of practical advice on self-propelled travel in the wilds of Mexico. If you find this book in a used book store, latch on to it!

The Real Guide: Mexico (1989), by John Fisher, Prentice-Hall, New York. In my opinion, this is one of the best of the mainstream tourist guides to Mexico. This book covers most of the country, and despite this vast area, it is surprisingly detailed and accurate.

APPENDIX B

SPEAKING SPANISH

Pronunciation Guide

When used before the Spanish letters *e* and *i*, the Spanish *c* is pronounced like the English *s*. For example, *el glaciar* (the glacier) is pronounced *el gla-see-AR*; *la cima* (the summit) is pronounced *la SEE-ma*. In all other cases, *c* is pronounced hard, like the English *k*.

Before the Spanish letters *e* and *i*, *g* is pronounced like the English *h*; in all other cases it is pronounced hard, like the English *g* in "good." For example, *el refugio* (the hut) is pronounced *el ray-FOO-hee-oh* and *el albergue* (the hut) is pronounced *el al-BER-gay*.

In Spanish, *h* is never pronounced. *Helar* (to freeze), for example, is pronounced *ay-LAR*.

The Spanish *j* is pronounced like the English *h*. *La Joya* (the jewel), for example, is pronounced *la HO-ya*.

The Spanish consonant *ll* is usually pronounced like the English *y*, as in *llano* (plain), pronounced *YA-no*.

The Spanish *y* is pronounced like the y in *yet*, never as the *y* in *only*. For example, *la joya* is pronounced *la HO-ya*.

The *ñ* in Spanish is similar to the *ny* in *canyon*. For example, *la cañada* (the ravine) is pronounced *la can-YA-da*.

The group of letters *que* is pronounced as *kay*.

The Spanish *z* is always pronounced like the English *s*. *Los zapatos* (the shoes) is pronounced *los sa-PAH-toes*.

Place Names

Abanico (ah-bah-NEE-ko)
Acatzingo (ah-caht-SEEN-go)
Agujas (ah-GOO-has)
Amacuilecatl (ah-ma-coo-WEE-la-catl)
Amecameca (ah-meh-kah-MEH-kah)
Antigua Flor (an-TEE-gwa flor)
Apizaco (ah-PEES-ah-ko)
Arista de Luz (ah-REES-tah day loos)
Arista del Sol (ah-REES-tah del sol)
Atenquique (ah-ten-KEE-kay)
Augusto Pellet (ow-GOOS-toe PAY-yay)

Ayoloco (aye-yo-LOW-co)
Balderas (bal-DAIR-as)
Barriga (ba-REE-ga)
Cabellera (kah-bay-YAIR-ah)
Cabeza (ka-BAY-sa)
Cañada Nahualac (can-YAH-da nah-WAL-ak)
Chalchoapan (chal-cho-A-pan)
Chalco (CHAL-co)
Cholula (cho-LOO-la)
Circuito Interior (sir-KWEE-to een-tay-REE-or)
Citlaltépetl (see-tlal-TAPE-etl)
Coscomatepec (cos-co-ma-TAPE-ec)
Cruces (KROO-says)
Cruz Roja (kroos RO-ha)
Cuello (KWAY-yo)
Cueva del Muerto (KWAY-va del MUWARE-to)
Ejercitio de Oriente (ay-hair-SEE-tee-o day oh-ree-EN-tay)
Glaciar de Jamapa (gla-see-AR day ha-MA-pa)
Glaciar Norte (gla-see-AR NOR-tay)
Glaciar Oriental (gla-see-AR oh-ree-en-TAL)
Grupo Alta Montaña (GROO-po AL-ta mon-TAHN-ya)
Huamantla (wah-MAHN-tlah)
Inescalables de la Cabellera (een-es-ka-LA-blays day la kah-bay-YAY-rah)
Iztaccíhuatl (ees-tay-SEE-watl)
Joya (HO-ya)
Malinche (mah-LEEN-chay)
Nexcoalanco (nay-co-ah-LAN-co)
Oreja Derecha (oh-RAY-ha day-RAY-cha)
Oreja Izquierda (oh-RAY-ha ees-kee-AIR-da)
Pared Norte (pah-RED NOR-tay)
Pecho (PAY-cho)
Pico del Aguila (PEE-ko del AH-gee-la)
Pico del Fraile (PEE-ko del FRA-ee-lay)
Pico de Orizaba (PEE-ko day oh-ree-SAH-bah)
Pico Mayor (PEE-ko ma-YOR)
Piedra Grande (pee-AY-dra GRAN-day)
Pies (PEE-ays)
Popocatépetl (po-po-ka-TAPE-etl)
Portillo (por-TEE-yo)
Pueblo Nuevo (PWAY-blo NWAY-vo)
Querétano (kay-air-AY-ta-no)
Rodillas (ro-DEE-yas)
Ruta del Sol (ROO-ta del sole)

Ruta Sur Occidente (ROO-ta sur ok-see-DEN-tay)
San Martín Texmelúcan (san mar-TEEN tay-mel-OO-kahn)
Sarcófago (sar-CO-fah-go)
Sultepec (sul-TAPE-ek)
Tenochtitlán (tay-nock-teet-LAN)
Teopixcalco (tay-oh-PEEX-cal-co)
Texcalco (tay-CAL-co)
Teyotl (tay-OTL)
Tlachichuca (tla-chi-CHOO-ka)
Tlalmanalco (tlal-mahn-AL-ko)
Tlamacas (tla-MAK-as)
Tlaxcala (tlas-KAH-la)
Torrecillas (tor-ray-SEE-yas)
Vicente Guerrero (vee-SEN-tay ge-RARE-roh)
Ventorrillo (ven-to-REE-yo)
Zoapan (so-AH-pan)

Climbing and Traveler's Vocabulary

Please note that the following words are in common use in Mexico and Spain, where the mountaineering vocabulary has its origins in the French language. Other Spanish-speaking countries (such as Argentina or Chile) more commonly use climbing words that are German in origin. So, an ice axe in Mexico is a *piolet* while in Argentina it is a *pickel*. Please keep this in mind when using this vocabulary in countries other than Mexico.

the abyss	*el abismo*	ah-BEES-mo
alpinism	*alpinismo*	al-pee-NEES-mo
the alpinist	*el alpinista*	al-pee-NEES-ta (masculine)
	la alpinista	al-pee-NEES-ta (feminine)
the arete	*la arista*	ah-REES-ta
to arrive	*llegar*	yay-GAR
(at the summit)	*(a la cumbre)*	(ah la KOOM-bray)
the ascent	*la subida*	soo-BEE-da
the avalanche	*el alud*	ah-LOOD
	la avalancha	ah-va-LAN-cha
the bargaining	*el regateo*	ray-ga-TAY-o
the belay	*el asegurado*	ah-say-goo-RAH-doe
	el amarrado	ah-ma-RAH-doe
to belay	*asegurar (to secure)*	ah-say-goo-RAR
	amarrar (to anchor)	ah-ma-RAR
the bergschrund	*la rimaya*	reem-AY-ah
the bindings	*las ataduras*	ah-tah-DOO-ras

the bivouac	*la vivaque*	vee-VAH-kay
the blizzard	*la ventisca*	ven-TEES-ka
the bolt	*la pitonisa*	pee-ton-EE-sa
the boots	*las botas*	BO-tahs
the large bottle	*el garrafón*	ga-rah-FON
the buttress	*el contrafuerte*	kon-trah-fu-AIR-tay
the cairn	*la pirca*	peer-KAH
the camp	*el campamento*	kam-pa-MEN-to
(high)	*(alto)*	(AL-to)
the candle	*la vela*	VAY-la
the carabiners	*los mosquetones*	mos-kay-TONE-ays
the chimney	*la chimenea*	chee-may-NAY-a
to chimney up	*deshollinar*	day-so-yee-NAR
the climb	*la subida*	soo-BEE-dah
to climb	*subir*	soo-BEER
the climber	*el escalador*	es-ka-la-DOR (masculine)
	la escaladora	es-ka-la-DOR-ah (feminine)
the cloud	*la nube*	NOO-bay
the col	*el cuello*	KWAY-yo
the compass	*el ámbito*	AM-bee-toe
the cornice	*la cornisa*	kor-NEE-sa
the couloir	*el colador*	ko-la-DOR
the crack	*le hendedura*	en-day-DOO-rah
the crampons	*los grampones*	gram-PON-ays
the crevasse	*la grieta*	gree-AY-ta
danger	*peligro*	pay-LEE-gro
the descent	*la bajada*	bah-HA-da
the dihedral	*el diedro*	dee-AY-dro
east	*este, oriente*	ES-tay, o-ree-EN-tay
exposed	*expuesto*	eks-PWAY-sto
the flashlight	*la linterna*	leen-TAIR-na
	eléctrica	ay-LEK-tree-ka
flat	*llano*	YA-no
the foam pad	*el colchón de esponja*	kol-CHON day ays-PON-ha
the fog	*la niebla*	nee-ABE-la
the food (provisions)	*los comestibles*	ko-mays-TEE-blays
frozen	*congelado*	kon-hay-LAD-oh
the gaiters	*las polainas*	po-LA-ee-nas
the gasoline	*la gasolina*	gas-o-LEEN-a
(white)	*blanca*	BLAN-ka
	la nafta	NAFF-ta
	la bencina	ben-SEE-na
the glacier	*el glaciar*	gla-see-AR
the gloves	*los guantes*	GWAN-tays
the guide	*el guía*	GEE-ah

the hammer	el martillo	mar-TEE-yo
the hardware store	la ferretería	fay-ray-tay-REE-ah
the headwall	la placa	PLA-kah
height	altura	al-TOO-ra
the helmet	el casco	KAS-ko
HELP!	¡SOCORRO!	so-KO-ro
high	alto	AL-to
the highways	las carreteras	ka-ray-TAY-ras
the hut	la cabaña	ka-BAN-ya
	el refugio	ray-FOO-he-o
	el albergue	al-BAIR-gay
the ice	el hielo	ee-AY-lo
the ice axe	el piolet	pee-o-LAY
the ice field	el banco de helado	BAN-ko day ay-LAD-oh
the ice hammer	el martillo de hielo	MAR-TEE-yo day ee-AY-lo
the ice piton	la clavija de hielo	kla-VEE-ha day ee-AY-lo
icy	helado	ay-LAD-oh
the jacket	la chaqueta	cha-KAY-ta
(down)	(de plumón)	(day ploo-MONE)
to jump	saltar	sal-TAR
the kerosene	el petróleo	pay-TRO-lay-o
the knife	el cuchillo	koo-CHEE-yo
(pocket)	(de bolsillo)	(day bol-SEE-yo)
the map	el mapa	MA-pa
(topographic map)	(carta topográfica)	(toe-po-GRA-fee-ka)
the matches	los fósforos	FOS-fo-ros
the moraine	la morena	mor-RAY-na
the mountaineer	el montañista	mone-tonn-YEES-ta (masc.)
	la montañista	mone-tonn-YEES-ta (fem.)
mountaineering	montañismo	mone-tonn-YEES-mo
(equipment)	el equipo de	ay-KEE-po day
	montañismo	mone-tonn-YEES-mo
the mountains	las montañas	mone-TONN-yas
(high)	(altas)	(AL-tas)
the mule driver	el arriero	ar-ree-AY-ro
north	norte	NOR-tay
the open book	el libro abierto	LEE-bro ah-bee-AIR-toe
the overboots	las cubrebotas	koo-bray-BO-tas
the pack	la mochila	mo-CHEE-la
the pack animals	las acémilas	ah-SAY-mee-las
the peak	el pico	PEE-ko
	el picacho	pee-KA-cho
the pitons	las clavijas	kla-VEE-has
the plateau	el altiplano	al-tee-PLA-no
the porter	el portador	por-ta-DOR

the precipice	*el precipicio*	pray-see-PEE-see-o
the rappel	*el rappel*	rap-PEL
the ravine	*la cañada*	kan-YA-da
	la garganta	gar-GAN-ta
to rent, charter	*rentar*	ren-TAR
	fletar	flay-TAR
the ridge	*el filo*	FEE-lo
the road	*el camino*	ka-MEE-no
ROCK!	*¡AGUAS!*[11]	AH-gwas
the rock	*la piedra*	pee-AY-dra
	la roca	RO-ka
the rockfall	*la caída de piedra*	ka-EE-da day pee-AY-dra
the rocks	*el terreno*[12]	teh-RAY-no
(loose)	*(suelto)*	(SWEL-toe)
(solid)	*(sólido)*	(SO-lee-doe)
the rope	*la cuerda*	KWAIR-da
	la soga	SO-ga
the rope team	*la cordada*	kor-DA-da
the route	*la ruta*	ROO-ta
the sand	*la arena*	ah-RAY-na
the scree	*el aluvión*	ah-loo-vee-OWN
to ski	*esquiar*	es-kee-AR
the ski poles	*los bastones*	bas-TONE-ays
the skis	*los esquís*	es-KEES
the sleeping bag	*el saco de dormir*	SA-ko day dor-MEER
the slope	*la pendiente*	pen-dee-YEN-tay
the snow	*la nieve*	nee-AY-vay
(new)	*(reciente)*	(ray-see-EN-tay)
(powder)	*(polvorosa)*	(pol-vo-ROS-ah)
the snowbridge	*el puente de nieve*	PWEN-tay day nee-AY-vay
the snow drift	*la ventisca*	ven-TEES-ka
south	*sud, sur*	sood, soor
steep	*escarpado*	es-kar-PA-doe
STOP!	*¡ALTO!*[13]	AL-to
	¡párese!	PAR-ay-say
the stove	*la estufa*	es-TOO-fa

---

11. This is a Mexican idiomatic expression. The literal translation is "waters."
Equivalent American expressions are "Watch your step!" and "Heads Up!"
Outside of the mountains, "¡Aguas!" is most frequently yelled at children who
loiter around gas stations.
12. This literally means "terrain." "La piedra suelta" would mean a rock that is not
bolted down, as opposed to what we would call a loose rock. So the use of
"terreno" is correct idiomatically but not literally.
13. Another idiomatic expression.

the stream	*la corriente*	ko-ree-EN-tay
the summit	*la cumbre*	KOOM-bray
	la cima	SEE-ma
the sunglasses	*las gafas oscuras*	GA-fas os-KOO-ras
the supermarket	*el supermercado*	soo-pair-mair-KAH-doe
the sweater	*el suéter*	SWAY-tair
the talus	*el talud*	ta-LOOD
the tent	*la tienda*	tee-EN-da
the trail	*el sendero*	sen-DAY-ro
to traverse	*atravesar*	ah-tra-vay-SAR
the tumpline	*la mecate*	may-KAH-tay
the valley	*el valle*	VA-yay
the village	*el pueblo*	PWAY-blo
the (rock) wall	*el muro*	MOO-row
the water	*el agua*	AH-gwa
(purified)	*(purificado)*	(poo-ree-fee-KAH-doe)
the water bottle	*la botella de agua*	bo-TAY-ya day AH-gwa
west	*oeste, occidente*	o-WES-tay, ok-see-DEN-tay
the wind	*el viento*	vee-EN-toe
the windbreaker	*el rompeviento*	rom-pay-vee-EN-toe
to zigzag up	*subir en zigzag*	soo-BEER en zig-zag

Climbing Phrases

Please show me the road to…	*Enséñeme el camino a…*
Where does this road lead?	*¿A dónde va este camino?*
Is it paved or is it dirt?	*¿Está pavimentado o está de tierra?*
Continue straight ahead.	*Siga adelante.*
What village is this?	*¿Qué pueblo es éste?*
Turn right (left).	*Da una vuelta a la derecha (izquierda).*
Is there a guide in the village?	*¿Hay algún guía en el pueblo?*
How far is it to… ?	*¿Como tan lejos está… ?*
We would like to climb the mountain tomorrow.	*Quisiéramos subir la montaña mañana.*
Can we get to… before dark?	*¿Podemos llegar a… antes de la noche?*
Crampons are essential.	*Son esenciales los grampones.*
Will I need a rope and an ice axe?	*¿Voy a necesitar una cuerda y un piolet?*
The climb is very steep.	*La subida es muy escarpada.*
You will need ice pitons when climbing the face.	*Necesitará usted clavijas de hielo para subir por la pared.*
Beware of the crevasses.	*Cuidado con las grietas.*

We will have to spend the night
in a mountain hut.

*Tendremos que pasar la noche
en algún refugio.*

We might lose our way in
the blizzard.

*Pudiéramos extraviarnos en
la ventisca.*

Do you like mountaineering?

¿Le gusta usted el montañismo?

You will become snow-blind if
you don't use your goggles.

*Le va a cegar el reflejo de la nieve,
si no pone las gafas oscuras.*

Can you let me have some cream
for sunburn?

*¿Me puede dejar usted la crema
contra la quemadura de sol?*

Did you have an easy climb
yesterday?

¿Tuvo usted una subida fácil ayer?

We reached the summit at noon.

Llegamos a la cumbre al mediodía.

What mountains are there in
this region?

*¿Cuales montañas hay en
esta región?*

Can we rent pack animals here?

Podemos rentar aquí las acémilas?

Is the price fixed?

¿Es un precio fijo?

Have you done any climbing?

¿Ha escalado usted antes?

The new snow is not good
for climbing.

*La nieve reciente no es buena para
subir.*

I must adjust my crampon
bindings.

*Tengo que ajustarme las ataduras
de los grampones.*

I don't like the snow; it is
dangerous.

*No me gusta la nieve; es
peligrosa.*

The snow has frozen overnight.

*La nieve se ha helado durante la
noche.*

Emergency Phrases

There has been an accident
on the mountain.

*Había un accidente
en la montaña.*

Send for a doctor.

Mande buscar un médico.

Send for the mountain rescue team.

*Mande buscar el equipo de
salvamiento.*

What is the matter with you?

¿Qué le ocurre a usted?

I don't feel well.

No me encuentro bien.

I feel very ill.

Me siento muy mal.

I am nauseated.

Me da naúsea.

I feel weak.

Me siento débil.

He (she) is suffering from
pneumonia (pulmonary edema).

*El (ella) está enfermo (enferma)
de pulmonía (edema pulmonar).*

He (she) must be taken to the
hospital.

*Hay que llevarle (llevarla) al
hospital.*

Is your digestion all right?

¿Está su digestíon bien?

He (she) has broken his (her) arm.

El (ella) se ha roto el brazo.

He (she) has fractured his (her) skull.	*El (ella) se ha fracturado el cráneo.*
You have had a bad concussion.	*Ha tenido usted una conmoción seria.*
I am injured.	*Estoy herido.*
Have you sprained your ankle?	*¿Se ha torcido un tobillo?*
He (she) is snow-blind.	*El (ella) está ciego (ciega) del reflejo de la nieve.*
Your foot is frostbitten.	*Su pie está túmido.*
The injured climbers were brought down on stretchers.	*Bajaron en camillas los montañistas heridos.*
They lost their way and a rescue party set out to find them.	*Se extraviaron y un equipo de socorro salió a buscarlos.*
A mountaineer was injured (died) in a fall.	*Un montañista se hirió (murió) en una caída.*
We will need a stretcher.	*Necesitamos una camilla.*
He (she) cannot walk.	*El (ella) no puede caminar.*
Please help us!	*¡Por favor, ayudénos!*
We need help.	*Necesitamos ayuda.*

APPENDIX C

EQUIPMENT LIST

This list indicates the equipment I have taken to the volcanoes in the early 1990s. This list will probably change as equipment improves, and as mountaineering styles and fads change.

CLOTHING

wool socks (three pair)
shorts
pile jacket
neck gaiter
sun hat
glove liners
gaiters

long underwear, tops and bottoms
wind pants
windbreaker, waterproof/breathable
warm cap
dark glasses
outer gloves

CLIMBING GEAR

mountaineering boots
crampons
carabiners
pulleys
165 feet of 9mm rope

ice axe
harness
runners
prusik slings

CAMPING EQUIPMENT

knapsack
sunscreen
three (3) one-liter water bottles
altimeter
toothbrush, toothpaste, soap
lightweight tarp/tent
foam pad
headlamp
cigarette lighter
fuel container
water-purification supplies

duffel bag
lip balm
compass
first-aid kit
plastic groundcloth
lightweight sleeping bag
cup and spoon
candles
gasoline stove
cooking pot

OTHER GEAR

notebooks, pens, pencils
roadmaps
padlock

Spanish–English dictionary
guidebooks
two cameras (one for color,
    one for black and white)

APPENDIX D
METRIC CONVERSIONS

METERS TO FEET

1 meter = 3.28 feet
5600 meters = 18,373 feet
5500 meters = 18,045 feet
5400 meters = 17,717 feet
5300 meters = 17,389 feet
5200 meters = 17,061 feet
5100 meters = 16,733 feet
5000 meters = 16,405 feet
4900 meters = 16,076 feet
4800 meters = 15,748 feet
4700 meters = 15,420 feet
4600 meters = 15,092 feet
4500 meters = 14,764 feet
4400 meters = 14,436 feet
4300 meters = 14,108 feet
4200 meters = 13,780 feet
4100 meters = 13,452 feet
4000 meters = 13,124 feet
3900 meters = 12,795 feet
3800 meters = 12,467 feet
3700 meters = 12,139 feet
3600 meters = 11,811 feet
3500 meters = 11,483 feet
3400 meters = 11,155 feet
3300 meters = 10,827 feet
3200 meters = 10,498 feet
3100 meters = 10,171 feet
3000 meters = 9,843 feet
2900 meters = 9,515 feet
2800 meters = 9,187 feet
2700 meters = 8,858 feet
2600 meters = 8,530 feet
2500 meters = 8,202 feet
2400 meters = 7,874 feet
2300 meters = 7,546 feet
2200 meters = 7,218 feet
2100 meters = 6,890 feet
2000 meters = 6,562 feet

FEET TO METERS

18,500 feet = 5639 meters
18,250 feet = 5562 meters
18,000 feet = 5486 meters

17,750 feet = 5410 meters
17,500 feet = 5333 meters
17,250 feet = 5257 meters
17,000 feet = 5181 meters
16,750 feet = 5105 meters
16,500 feet = 5029 meters
16,250 feet = 4952 meters
16,000 feet = 4876 meters
15,750 feet = 4800 meters
15,500 feet = 4724 meters
15,250 feet = 4648 meters
15,000 feet = 4571 meters
14,750 feet = 4495 meters
14,500 feet = 4419 meters
14,250 feet = 4343 meters
14,000 feet = 4267 meters
13,750 feet = 4191 meters
13,500 feet = 4115 meters
13,250 feet = 4039 meters
13,000 feet = 3962 meters
12,750 feet = 3886 meters
12,500 feet = 3810 meters
12,250 feet = 3734 meters
12,000 feet = 3657 meters
11,750 feet = 3581 meters
11,500 feet = 3505 meters
11,250 feet = 3439 meters
11,000 feet = 3352 meters
10,750 feet = 3276 meters
10,500 feet = 3200 meters
10,250 feet = 3124 meters
10,000 feet = 3047 meters
9,750 feet = 2971 meters
9,500 feet = 2895 meters
9,250 feet = 2819 meters
9,000 feet = 2743 meters
8,750 feet = 2666 meters
8,500 feet = 2590 meters
8,250 feet = 2514 meters
8,000 feet = 2438 meters
7,750 feet = 2362 meters
7,500 feet = 2285 meters
7,250 feet = 2210 meters
7,000 feet = 2133 meters

INDEX